CONSERVATISM

CONSERVATISM

DREAM
and
REALITY

Robert Nisbet

With a new introduction by
Brad Lowell Stone

Transaction Publishers
New Brunswick (U.S.A.) and London (U.K.)

Fourth printing 2008

New material this edition copyright © 2002 by Transaction Publishers, New Brunswick, New Jersey 08903. Originally published in 1986 by University of Minnesota Press.

This book is printed on acid-free paper that meets the American National Standard for Permanence of Paper for Printed Library Materials.

Library of Congress Catalog Number: 2001041454
ISBN: 978-0-7658-0862-2
Printed in the United States of America

Library of Congress Cataloging-in-Publication Data
Nisbet, Robert A.
   Conservatism: dream and reality / Robert Nisbet
        p. cm.
   Originally published: Minneapolis: University of Minnesota Press, c1986, in series: Concepts in social thought.
With new introd.
   Includes bibliographical references and index.
   ISBN 0-7658-0862-5 (pbk. : alk. paper)
        1. Conservatism. 1. Title.

JC573 .N57 2001
320.52'09—dc21   2001041454

Contents

Introduction to the Transaction Edition

The republication of Robert Nisbet's *Conservatism: Dream and Reality* is a wonderful event, and the book is an ideal addition to the Library of Conservative Thought. Concerning the book, Russell Kirk said that "people may desire to commence their serious study of conservative thought by reading a succinct but sensible manual on the subject. If so, I commend particularly an agreeably slim volume by Robert A. Nisbet, entitled simply *Conservatism: Dream and Reality....*" [1] Of course, Kirk knew something of which he spoke. He was the dean of American conservatism and the author of *The Conservative Mind*, the book that incited the post-World War II conservative intellectual movement in America.

I cannot hope to match Kirk's credentials or outdo his recommendation. Nor need I in introducing this volume draw attention to implicit themes or illuminate difficult passages. The book is beautifully written and perfectly accessible. What I can do is show how this little book fits within the corpus of Nisbet's work and briefly appraise Nisbet's legacy. Regarding the relationship of *Conservatism: Dream and Reality* to Nisbet's other writings, I will highlight several among many points of continuity. Also worthy of comment, however, is the fact that the form of "liberalism" to which Nisbet directs his animus below differs from the liberalism criticized in his previous works. Herein, liberalism is chiefly Benthamite and Millian liberalism, not "classical liberalism." Indeed, Adam Smith is acknowledged to have been Edmund Burke's "cherished friend" and is treated sympathetically (51, 75-76). Similarly, in the introduction to *The Making of Modern Society*, published along with the first edition of *Conservatism: Dream and Reality* in 1986, Nisbet praised for the first time other classical liberals such as John Locke, the Baron de Montesquieu and David Hume. [2] This change, I believe, is worth noting for reasons that go beyond the interests of scholars. For Nisbet's changed view may suggest the way by which a rapprochement is

1

possible between two often antagonistic camps of contemporary conservatives—traditionalists and those who claim inspiration from classical liberalism.

I

His shifting view of classical liberalism aside, Nisbet was nothing if not consistent over the course of his long and productive career. The essential concerns of *Conservatism: Dream and Reality* are the same as those of his first and most influential book, *The Quest for Community* (1953), although as Nisbet records below his first book was "not particularly written...as a conservative book" (106). In fact, the theme that unites virtually all of Nisbet's writings is announced in the preface to *The Quest for Community*. He states there, "I have chosen to deal with the *political* causes of the manifold alienations that lie behind the contemporary quest for community." [3] The sovereign political state, he believed, is more than a legal relationship or a superstructure of power. "The real significance of the modern state is inseparable from its successive penetrations of man's economic, religious, kinship and local allegiances, and its revolutionary dislocations of established centers of function and authority." [4]

Nisbet maintained throughout his career that individual estrangement and the ardent modern desire for communal fellowship result from the erosion of intermediate communities produced by the Western political state.

Nisbet states below that political philosophies or ideologies are typically conceived in terms of their views of the relationship of the individual and the state. A more useful approach, he insists, includes "the structure of groups and associations which are intermediate to the two polar entities" (37). In a word, what is often missing is a concern for the "social." As Nisbet observes in *Prejudices* (1982), the term "social" is a coinage of the nineteenth century in which an ancient term was given new meaning. "Social, as a word, meant family, village, parish, town, voluntary association, and class, not the political state."[5] Society is comprised of the communities—social groups, associations and institutions—mediating the relationship between the individual and the state, and it exists in an inverse relationship with both the individual and the state, according to Nisbet. The individual and the state are mutually sustaining poles, not opposites, because the state is essential to securing individual rights and because the "loose individual's" quest for community often embraces the absolute communal state as the highest form of community. Both the individual and the state, however, are opposed to society.

The concentration of power within the state and the separation of individuals from society in the West have occurred by fits and starts over the last five hundred years, according to Nisbet. Given the abundance of medieval communities there was no conscious crisis of community in the Middle Ages. The group was primary. By contrast, the foremost modern problem, Nisbet says, is the problem of community—"community lost, and community to be gained."[6] Certainly, no other term in the Nisbetian lexicon is as important as "community." He uses the word concretely. Communities are not maintained by sentiment, at least not alone. Rather, communities arise to address basic human needs and to solve problems. As Nisbet says, quoting Ortega y Gassett, "Human beings do not come together to *be* together; they come together to *do something* together."[7] Specifically, in *The Degradation of Academic Dogma* (1970), Nisbet identifies several ideal-typical attributes of communities. He says every community has a *function* it fulfills; a *dogma* or transcending purpose; *authority* that is established through habit, custom, use, and wont; a *hierarchy* of status and roles; a sense of *honor* that transcends the merely pecuniary or utilitarian; and a feeling of *superiority* that helps distance the community from its environs.[8] The range of communities includes those of kinship, locale, conscience, ethnicity, fraternity, scholarship, recreation, occupation, mutual-aid and voluntary association.

Their essential features make communities vulnerable in our age. As Nisbet observes below, the "icy rationalism" of reformers such as Jeremy Bentham leads them to distrust habitual or customary authority (57). Moreover, the parochialism and particularism of communities are often seen as unfortunate covers for unsavory prejudice and exclusivity; secularism degrades all dogma; the hierarchy of communities offends the egalitarian ethos; the sense of superiority of communities is taken as arrogance; the cash nexus makes honor appear foolish; and the state is considered a more equitable and efficient provider of social functions than communities. Nonetheless, Nisbet says that historically war has been the prime occasion and means for the state to aggrandize its power at the expense of communities. Traditional communities are pluralistic, concentric and independent. During times of war, the state must individualize them and neutralize their authority. "To the military function is added in time other functions of a legal, juridical, economic, and even religious nature, and, over a long period, we can see the passage of the State from an exclusively military association to one incorporating every aspect of human life."[9] Thus, Nisbet says, the war-state is the main source of the welfare-state. *In Twilight of Authority* (1975) he estimated that 75 percent of all national programs in the West over the last two hundred years to equalize income, property and opportunity "have been in the first instance adjuncts of war and the war economy."[10] It is for this reason that below Nisbet says that of all the misapplications of the term "conservative" in the last few decades none is more amusing than the application of the term to militarists (111). Elsewhere, Nisbet says flatly, "the military spirit and conservatism have nothing in common." [11]

Communities are the substance of society, and, as Nisbet makes clear in *Conservatism: Dream and Reality*, "the sole object of the conservative tradition is the protection of the social order and its constitutive groups from the enveloping bureaucracy of the national state." [12] Nisbet argues at great length in *The Sociological Tradition* (1966) in fact that the field of sociology arose from ground cleared by conservatives such as Burke in their defense of traditional society against the French Revolutionaries. As Nisbet states below, in the aftermath of the Revolution words such as *"social, tradition, custom, institution, folk, community, organism, tissue* and *collective* achieved almost overnight a prestige and function they had not known since the heyday of realist vs. nominalist thought in the Middle Ages" (86). By virtue of their lament-filled eulogy of the world of social institutions, conservatives identified this world for study by nineteenth-century sociologists. Indeed, Nisbet says in *The Sociological Tradition* that while most golden age sociologists were not particularly conservative in their overt political commitments, it is still possible to see in Durkheim, Simmel and Weber "deep currents of conservatism." [13] Conservatism more than liberalism or radicalism, Nisbet believed, lies at the root of sociology. As he puts within these pages, "More of the spirit of Burke is to be found in the thinking of Durkheim and Weber on the nature of society than of, say Voltaire, Diderot— or Bentham" (88).

According to Nisbet, one of the consequences of the rediscovery of the social in the nineteenth century was that the Western idea of progress was transformed. He says in *Conservatism: Dream and Reality* that in the eighteenth century "the epochs of the past by which the advancement of mankind was measured were commonly intellectual or cultural" but in the nineteenth century they were "social" (87). Nineteenth-century views of social order and change typically assumed that the principle of progress was inherent or immanent within society itself. In such "developmental" philosophies of history, change was deemed natural, directional, continuous and cumulative, and, Nisbet says, for much of the last two centuries developmentalism was embraced so widely that the idea of progress became something of a popular religion. "Progress has been in a great many quarters the precise equivalent in spiritual terms of Providence" (97).

Nisbet investigated "developmentalism" in two books, *Social Change and History* (1969) and *History of the Idea of Progress* (1980). As one might imagine, Nisbet's conservatism made him doubt the root assumptions of developmentalism. He argued that social change is episodic, contingent and results from extraordinary extrinsic causes, not from uniform intrinsic causes. [14] What might surprise is that although he doubted the validity of developmentalism as a description of history, Nisbet lamented the current moribund state of the idea of progress because the *idea* of progress has been "a powerful intellectual force behind Western civilization's spectacular achievements" and because the idea links people to the past and future. [15]

In self-conscious opposition to economic determinism, Nisbet always stressed the *causal* role of ideas in human affairs. "Everything vital in history," he says, "reduces itself ultimately to ideas, which are the motive forces. Man *is* what he *thinks*." [16] Accordingly, Nisbet's works contain a history of those ideas that have aided, mirrored or combated the displacement of communities by the political state. In several books, including *Twilight of Authority* and *The Social Philosophers* (1982), this history is cast in terms of two great traditions in Western thought: political monism and social pluralism. "In the first, which begins with Plato, the political state is given an emphasis that virtually extinguishes other forms of association. Hobbes, Rousseau, Bentham, Michelet, Fitche, Treitschke are among principals in this tradition, which includes, of course, the numberless members of the political clerisy of our own day." Within political monism "[s]uch groups as family, locality, neighborhood, church and other autonomous associations are almost uniformly reduced to their individual atoms, made into units dependent upon concession of existence by the state, or in some other way significantly degraded." [17] The second tradition begins with Aristotle and includes such diverse thinkers as Aquinas, Bodin, Althusius, Burke, Tocqueville, Acton, Proudhon and Kropotkin. Social pluralism at various times, Nisbet observes below "could be taken up by conservative, liberal and radical causes alike" (62). For each of these pluralists, however, freedom proceeds "less from what the actual constitution of the political order proper may prescribe than from the relationship that exists between the political state, whatever the form of government, and the several institutions of the social sphere." For pluralists, a government cannot be free "if the powers of the state have reached out to encompass all spheres of social, moral, economic, and intellectual existence." [18]

Nisbet admired pluralism in its many forms but he saw Burke and Tocqueville as the two most important social pluralists. Burke and Tocqueville are also the two thinkers who most influenced Nisbet, as is amply clear in the pages that follow. Nisbet treated Hobbes and Rousseau as the two most seminal political monists; he regarded them as the "prime catalytic agents" in modern political thinking. The philosophy of both men, he said, is a "rigorous blend of social nihilism and political affirmation." [19] Both were contemptuous of society and both envisioned a state in service of the individual.

II

For most of his career Nisbet set classical liberalism against social pluralism. For example, in *The Quest for Community* he says "When the basic principles of modern liberalism were being formulated by such men as Locke, Montesquieu, Adam Smith, and Jefferson, the image of man luminous in the philosophical mind was an image constructed out of such traits as sovereign reason, stability, security, and indestructible motivations toward freedom and order. Man, abstract man, was deemed to be inherently self-suffing, equipped by nature with both the instincts and reason that could make him autonomous." He continues, "The philosophy of individualism became a rationalist psychology devoted to the ends of the release of man from the old and a sociology based upon the view that groups and institutions are at best mere reflections of the solid and ineffaceable fact of the individual." [20] Of Locke specifically, Nisbet says that he was "a derivative thinker. Hobbes was his master in all important respects." [21]

As noted above, Nisbet's views of classical liberalism had undergone a dramatic change by 1986. In *Conservatism: Dream and Reality*, Nisbet records Burke as asserting that government should limit its influence to "everything that is truly and properly public." Nisbet goes on, "But *not*, Burke emphasizes, to problems and necessities of the private sphere. In this there is not the slightest distinction between Burke and his friend Adam Smith." Indeed, Nisbet adds, "Despite the occasional intimations from time to time among self-styled Burkean conservatives that Burke followed a different drummer than Adam Smith, there is in fact no serious difference between them on the function of government" (51). And some pages later, Nisbet observes that Burke did not share in the "frequent criticism of capitalism" and that his views of commerce mirrored those of his "cherished friend Adam Smith" (75-76). Meanwhile, in *The Making of Modern Society*, Montesquieu is explicitly portrayed as a social pluralist. Nisbet says, "Montesquieu referred approvingly to the *corps intermediaires*, the historically-descended intermediate groups which he quite correctly saw as valuable reinforcements to the mixed system of government he prized. He saw them as the limits upon political power which they must always be...."[22] And, although Locke is linked to Hobbes below (19), both Locke and Hume are pictured in *The Making of Modern Society* as social pluralists laboring in opposition to the visions of monists such as Plato, Rousseau and Marx. Nisbet says, "In almost sole opposition to these visions are the ideas of Locke, Hume, the Founding Fathers, Burke, Tocqueville and their intellectual descendents who relish the plural, differentiated, particularistic and decentralized state in which the freedom of individuals is buttressed by the autonomy of all groups and associations which prevent man from becoming an inert particle in sandheap-mass."[23]

I believe the evidence supports the interpretations of classical liberalism found in *Conservatism: Dream and Reality* and *The Making of Modern Society*. Locke, Montesquieu, Hume and Smith must be counted among the most important and influential social pluralists.

For example, Montesquieu's discussions of "intermediate" or "secondary" groups kindled Tocqueville's interests, and the pluralistic structure of the American Constitution can be attributed at least in part to the influence of Hume and Montesquieu upon James Madison. How Nisbet failed to see the social pluralism of the classical liberals early in his career I am not certain, but I suspect that his view was reinforced by his taking seriously libertarian claims to be the intellectual heirs of classical liberalism. Certainly, Nisbet was very critical of libertarianism. [24] Nonetheless, the views of the classical liberals converge far more with those of Burke and Nisbet than they do with those libertarians who deem social authority as comparable to political authority and who dream of a world wherein all relationships are voluntary contracts. Consequently, I believe that a rapprochement between traditionalists and libertarians is possible if both understood that the classical liberals did not maintain a hedonistic, asocial view of human nature.

According to Locke, Montesquieu, Hume, and Smith, we are naturally social or communal. Our original circumstance was conjugal, familial, or tribal. Property was communal and individuals were devoted to their small bands. By virtue of this selfless devotion, however, these individuals were distrustful of strangers and hateful towards them. The original condition was not one of the war of all against all, as Hobbes claimed, according to the classical liberals. It was the war of some against some—a far bloodier war because it was fired by communal devotion. For the classical liberals, political society was the solution to the problem of selective devotion or innate partiality and to the related problem of conflicts over property. Within political society, as in our original condition, however, the reach of communal affection and obligation is *naturally* limited, and given the social and geographical extent of nation-states, the liberals distinguished between two realms within modern civil society— a communal private realm, and a public, primarily commercial realm. These two realms are arranged on very different principles. Whereas the private or familiar realm is founded on particularistic and selfless concern for the few, the public realm of commerce—like the state itself—is founded upon self-interest that is indifferent to the qualities of strangers. Whereas the private realm relies upon the original and natural sentiment of benevolence, the public realm relies upon justice as sustained by utilitarian reason. Whereas one's status in the private realm is largely ascribed and one's relationships are beyond contracts and codified rules, in the public arena one's relationships are contractual and rule-governed. And whereas the private or communal realm is improved by discrete, particularistic acts of benevolence, universal justice sustains public encounters systemically; exceptional or particularistic treatment is vicious because it destroys impartial justice. What is virtuous in one realm is vicious in the other.

The lengthy discussions of the private realm by the classical liberals are regularly neglected by critics. Such neglect may well account for Nisbet's early portrayal of Locke as an Hobbesian clone. Yet, Locke's *Second Treatise* treats the family and government in equal measure. According to Locke, the family exists in the "state of nature" and parents have both natural affection for their children and a non-contractual, unilateral obligation to raise those children to maturity, as dictated by natural law or reason. (The honor children award their parents is contingent upon the fulfillment of this natural duty.) For all the classical liberals, the private realm is at least as important as the public realm: it is the realm wherein selfless acts are nurtured, wherein we are regulated by the approbation and disapprobation of our intimates, and wherein we undertake positive acts aimed at common ends, genuine corporate acts.[25]

Misconceptions of the classical liberals necessarily follow from a failure to recognize their distinction between the private and public realms. One can imagine that Nisbet's early reading of the liberals resulted from his belief that classical liberal descriptions of public realm motives and actions reveal the whole of the classical liberal view of human nature and institutions. The same is also true of those libertarians who refer to classical liberalism in order to justify their own social atomism. Properly conceived, however, the views of the familiar realm, commerce and government maintained by Burke, the classical liberals, and Nisbet converge, and each of these thinkers must be seen as among the most important advocates of social pluralism.

III

Nisbet argued that in any form social pluralism has had little real presence within recent social scientific thinking; political monism, he believed, was the prevailing social scientific worldview. He asserted in fact that "given the extent to which all the social sciences have become monopolized by political values and aspirations, it would be more correct if they were called political sciences."[26] This is certainly true today. Most social scientists see economic conditions causing social ills, the perceived solutions to which are statist in nature. At the same time, however, political monism outside the social sciences has clearly waned over the last two decades or so. One pundit, in fact, asserted in the early 1990s that "Nisbetism" had become the "stated creed of American politics at the highest level."[27] Though exaggerated, this assertion contains a measure of truth. Among politicians in both major parties, public intellectuals, and average citizens, materialistic explanations of social problems and statist solutions to such problems have lost much of their appeal. The 1996 replacement of AFDC—"welfare" as we once knew it— by state and locally administered TANF programs is merely the most obvious instance of the retreat from federal bureaucracy to localism and social pluralism (although it is arguably also the most successful policy initiative of the last thirty-five years). By various measures we have seen at least the glimmerings of social replenishment in recent years. For example, "community policing" has contributed to declining crime rates, associational memberships probably have been increasing for some time, and, while divorce rates remain high, they have undergone a slow decline since the early 1980s.[28]

None of this would have surprised Nisbet. His tone was sometimes despairing but he believed that humans naturally possess a "social impulse"—an impulse to form groups— that fosters "social inventions." The history of social organization, he suggests, "comes down basically to the history of the rise and spread of social inventions."[29] For instance, the medieval period saw the creation of "monastery...village community, manor, fief, guild, university, [and] parish," while during the nineteenth century "mutual aid society in new forms, the consumers' and the producers' cooperatives, the assurance societies, the labor unions, and the business corporations were all without exception ingenious adaptions to problems presented by a new economic age."[30] Social reorganization and replenishment are as much a part of human history as periods of social disorganization and individual isolation.

Nisbet would not have been surprised by the recent indicators of social rejuvenation but he would still enjoin us to seek social pluralistic remedies for enduring social problems such as domestic vio-lence, long-term poverty, educational deficiencies, drug use, crum-bling inner-cities and the like. The available evidence sustains Nisbet's beliefs that such problems result not from economic condi-tions but from our faltering social infrastructure, especially—in these examples—from the unstable American family and that typically bureaucratic solutions have exacerbated the problems they were designed to ameliorate. Nisbet argued in the conclusions of both *The Quest for Community* and *Twilight of Authority* that what is re-quired to address such problems is a new "form of laissez-faire that has for its object, not the abstract individual, whether economic or political man, but rather the social group or association."[31] It is only through such conditions, Nisbet suggests, that "the human need for community [can] be met through ways other than politics—political action, political crusade, political Leviatian." [32]

Nisbet was accutely aware that vested interests within the national government itself and within much of the intellectual clerisy are for-midable obstacles to creating conditions facilitating social groups. Such interests are strongly committed to " the national community" and, according to Nisbet, combating such interests is essential to conservatism. In fact, according to *Conservatism: Dream and Real-ity*, antistatism and social pluralism are the two defining features of conservatism. As Nisbet asserted in one of his last essays, it should be the "prime business" of any conservative "to expose the fraudu-lence" of the phrase "national community" and any serious conser-vative person or group confronts a double task. "The first is to work tirelessly toward the diminution of the centralized, onmicomptent, and unitary state.... The second and equally important task is that of protecting, reinforcing, nurturing where necessary the varied groups and associations which form the true building blocks of the social order."[33]

Nisbet's antistatist and social pluralist conception of conserva-tism leads him in *Conservatism: Dream and Reality* to deny the la-bel of "conservative" to many who would claim it (110-114). In his view, although libertarians are reliably antistatist, they are not con-servatives because they are not social pluralists. Meanwhile, milita-rists, populists, and certain New Right enthusiasts are not conserva-tives because they seek to enhance the power of the state or to cap-ture the state in order to impose their moral vision. Nisbet concludes, in fact, that the coalition of the American Right is quite tenuous and not particularly conservative. Whatever their merits otherwise, these assertions contribute greatly to the health of conservatism because they compel conservatives to deliberate over the very purposes or ends informing their world view and directing their activities.

Brad Lowell Stone

Notes

1.   Russell Kirk, *The Politics of Prudence* (Bryn Mawr, PA: Intercollegiate Studies Institute, 1993), 49.
2.   Robert Nisbet, *The Making of Modern Society* (New York: NYU Press, 1986), 25, 28-29.
3.   Robert Nisbet, *The Quest for Community* (New York: Oxford University Press, 1953), vii.
4.   Ibid., viii.
5.   Robert Nisbet, *Prejudices: A Philosophical Dictionary* (Cambridge, MA: Harvard University Press, 1982), 287.
6.   Nisbet, *Quest*, vii.
7.   Robert Nisbet, *The Degradation of Academic Dogma: The University in America, 1945-1970* (New York: Basic Books, 1971), 43.
8.   Nisbet, *Dogma*, 41-56.
9.   Nisbet, *Quest*, 101.
10.   Robert Nisbet, *Twilight of Authority* (New York: Oxford University Press, 1975), 220.
11.   Nisbet, *Prejudices*, 60.
12.   Ibid., 59.
13.   Robert Nisbet, *The Sociological Tradition* (New York: Basic Books, 1966), 12.
14.   See Robert Nisbet, *Social Change and History* (New York: Oxford University Press, 1969), 270-304.
15.   See Robert Nisbet, *History of the Idea of Progress* (New York: Basic Book, 1980), 317-357.
16.   Nisbet, *Twilight*, 233.
17.   Ibid., 245.
18.   Ibid., 245-246.
19.   Robert Nisbet, *The Social Philosophers: Community and Conflict in Western Thought* (New York: Washington Square Press, 1982), 10.
20.   Nisbet, *Quest*, 225, 226.
21.   Ibid., 138
22.   Nisbet, *Modern Society*, 25.
23.   Ibid., 28-29
24.   On libertarianism see Robert Nisbet, "Uneasy Cousins" in *Freedom and Virtue: The Conservative/Libertarian Debate*, edited by George W. Carey (Wilmington, DE: ISI Books, 1998), 38-54.
25.   Among the essential texts of classical liberalism are John Locke, *Second Treatise of Government* (Indianapolis: Hackett, 1980); Montesquieu, *The Spirit of the Laws* trans. Anne Cohen, Basia Miller, Harold Stone (Cambridge: Cambridge University Press, 1989); David Hume, *A Treatise of Human Nature* (Oxford: Claredon Press,

1978) and *An Enquiry Concerning the Principles of Morals* (Indianapolis: Bobbs-Merrill, 1957); Adam Smith, *An Inquiry into the Nature and Causes of the Wealth of Nations* (Indianapolis: Liberty Press, 1981) and *The Theory of Moral Sentiments* (Indianapolis: Liberty Press, 1982). The brief discussion here of classical liberalism and Nisbet draws from a more elaborate discussion in my *Robert Nisbet: Communitarian Traditionalist* (Wilmington, DE: ISI Books, 2000), 114-124.

26.   Nisbet, *Prejudices*, 287.
27.   Nicholas Lemann, "Paradigm Lost," *The Washington Monthly* 23 (April, 1991), 46.
28.   See Everett Ladd, *The Ladd Report* (New York: Free Press, 1999) on associational memberships. Ladd refutes claims that associational memberships have been declining. See Robert Putnum, "Bowling Alone: America's Declining Social Capital," *Journal of Democracy* 6 (1995), 65-78. For a discussion of various indicators of social replenishment see Francis Fukuyama, *The Great Disruption* (New York: Free Press, 1999).
29.   Nisbet, *Twilight*, 276.
30.   Ibid., 281.
31.   Ibid., 276.
32.   Ibid. Also see Nisbet, *Quest*, 278-284.
33.   Robert Nisbet, "Still Questing," *The Intercollegiate Review*, 29 (Fall, 1993), 41-45.

Preface

Conservatism is one of the three major political ideologies of the past two centuries in the West, the other two being liberalism and socialism. I am aware that a few writers have eschewed use of the word 'ideology' for conservatism, apparently on the theory that this philosophy by its nature lacks the elements of activism and reform which supposedly go into a genuine ideology.

But this is to take a narrow and stunted view of the word 'ideology.' Leaving aside the historical meanings it has had, such as its pejorative reference to a certain class of ideas in Napoleonic times and its use by Marx for the collective consciousness of a social class, the sense of 'ideology' in our age is quite clear, and altogether useful. Stated briefly, an ideology is any reasonably coherent body of moral, economic, social and cultural ideas that has a solid and well known reference to politics and political power; more specifically a power base to make possible a victory for the body of ideas. An ideology, in contrast to a mere passing configuration of opinion, remains alive for a considerable period of time, has major advocates and spokesmen and a respectable degree of institutionalization. It is likely to have charismatic figures in its history—Burkes, Disraelis, Churchills, etc.—among conservatives and their counterparts in liberalism and socialism.

Any ideology conjures up associations with practical politics—the sphere of politicians, political parties, manifestoes, and laws passed—as well as books, articles and lectures. At first thought, we might be more inclined to go the first sphere than the second, the sphere of campaigns, elections, governments in power, and political speeches. But this is on balance deceptive, even treacherous. Naturally there is a relationship between practical politics and ideology, but there is no iron in the relationship, nothing to keep even the best disciplined party and its leaders ever faithful to the ideology. Emergencies, accidents, tactical decisions, may and often do lead to doc-

15

trinal apostasy. Since this is usually in the name of individual or party victory, it may not matter too much. There is, after all, one overriding objective for a political party: victory. Much the same holds for the individual politician, the serious one at any rate.

To try to derive the ideology from the decisions and acts of even the greatest of politicians more often than not leads to confusion. Not that ideologies are immutable and impervious to the buffets on them of men and events. But no politician lives by ideology alone; all are at once larger and smaller than the ideologies they represent. Like Anteus, the politician must come down to ideological soil occasionally, but we should never underestimate the temptations of power, of the desire to head off the opposition, and the impulse for revenge from time to time.

Lincoln's Emancipation Proclamation, Bismarck's instigation of unemployment insurance, Disraeli's turn to the reform bills of the 1870s, Churchill's embrace of the Liberals in 1909 and of bills against the aristocracy, even the use of liquor, and de Gaulle's stunning reversal of his own Algerian policy, all of these are bold strokes by lifelong conservatives. But to seek to force each of them into the reigning ideology of conservatism is absurd. It is to overlook the well-recorded play on every great politician's mind of deep desires of self or imperatives of country.

Disraeli spoke to the point:

> The truth is, gentlemen, a statesman is the creature of his age, the child of circumstances, the creation of his times. A statesman is essentially a practical character; and when he is called upon to take office, he is not to inquire what his opinion might or might not have been on this or that subject; he is only to ascertain the needful and the beneficial, and the most feasible measure to be carried out.

Churchill observed that 'true patriotism sometimes requires of men to act contrary, at one period, to that which it does at another.' Sheer personal drive, in a word, egoism, is never to be disregarded. What Beaverbrook said of Lloyd George is always pertinent: 'He doesn't care which direction he rides so long as he has full rein.' Robespierre is credited with 'Perish the colonies rather than a principle.' But no true political leader, no Cromwell, Lincoln, de Gaulle, or other would speak such nonsense.

Where, then, do we go for the substance of an ideology. Thirty years ago, T.S. Eliot, in a lecture on literature and politics,[1] provided sufficient answer, it seems to me, for conservatism or any other ideology. Eliot said that the nature of practical politics compels us to go to a different stratum of resources, a stratum that Eliot, following his friend V. A. Demant, called the 'pre–political.' This, said Eliot, is the 'stratum down to which any sound political thinking must push its roots and from which it must derive nourishment.' It is the stratum that is created over a considerable period of time by a diversity of people, social critics, political philosophers, essayists, even highly practical politicians themselves. What they have in common is commitment to a large political objective, of the kind best represented in the West by liberalism, conservatism and socialism. Eliot stated that normally there will be a 'gradation of types between thought and action', at one extreme the contemplative, at the other 'the N.C.O. of politics;' in between these two extremes lies the 'pre–political.'

My essential concern in this book is the 'pre–political' of modern conservatism, though not to the absolute neglect of the political. I deal for the most part with a tradition of political thought that stretches from Edmund Burke down to such contemporaries as Russell Kirk, Michael Oakeshott and Bertrand de Jouvenel. It is, of course, the ideas and values shared, the tenets and dogmas of political thought which matter most in a book of this sort, not the personalities and immediate surroundings of the major characters. This book is not a work in the history of conservatism, but rather in the anatomy of the ideology or, as I call it in Chapter 2, the dogmatics. What is important for my purposes are the arching perspectives, the essential insights and propositions, and the intellectual thrusts of conservatism as this body of thought has existed in the West for nearly 200 years.

I have aimed at the elements of conservatism which seem to me not only important but also distinctive when seen against the background formed by other ideologies. It may be true to call conservatism the 'politics of liberty' or 'the search for political virtue,' to take two recent characterizations, but we are not greatly advantaged, it seems to me, when, rightly or wrongly, liberalism and socialism might with equal warrant so describe themselves. I have sought therefore the themes which are at once distinctive in conservatism and which have had demonstrable continuity over the last 200 years.

Citations from the more prominent philosophers of conservatism are offered more for flavor than substance. I have deliberately avoided any chronological placement of these for, as noted, this is not a history but an anatomy of conservatism, and what is chiefly important,

I think, is simply reminder that a given major theme of conservatism enjoys as much currency today as it did a century or more ago. I have cited from Burke more than anyone else: this is proper and indeed inevitable. Burke is the prophet—the Marx or the Mill—of conservatism, and it is a mark of his continuing prophetic status that he has been cited and otherwise recognized by conservatives during the last quarter of a century in Britain and America in a degree greater than in any comparable period before. It is the essence of a major ideology, as of a religion or theology, to stress continuity and consistency. Sciences seek constantly to go beyond their founders, but ideologies do not. That is why Burke would have little difficulty in conversing today with the Jouvenels, Kirks and Oakeshotts of the 'pre–political,' and also with the Thatchers and Reagans of the 'political strata.'

Note

1.   *The Literature of Politics (1955),* published by The Conservative Political Centre, London.

1

Sources of Conservatism

Conservatism did not become a part of political speech until about 1830 in England. But its philosophical substance was brought into being in 1790 by Edmund Burke in his *Reflections on the Revolution in France*. Rarely in the history of thought has a body of ideas been as closely dependent upon a single man and a single event as modern conservatism is upon Edmund Burke and his fiery reaction to the French Revolution. In remarkable degree, the central themes of conservatism over the last two centuries are but widenings of themes enunciated by Burke with specific reference to revolutionary France.

He himself was clearly aware that the French Revolution was at bottom a European revolution, but that truth had to await the writings of such ardent traditionalists as Bonald, de Maistre, and Tocqueville for its detailed statement. In Burke and in them we find the outlines of a philosophy of history that was the diametric opposite of the Whig or progressive philosophy; and we find too a perspicuous statement of the importance of feudalism and of other historically grown structures such as patriarchal family, local community, church, guild and region which, under the centralizing, individualizing influence of natural law philosophy, had almost disappeared from European political thought in the seventeenth and eighteenth centuries. In the writing of Hobbes, Locke and Rousseau, traditional society and its historically evolved groups and traditions was recognized dimly at best, almost always with hostility. What alone was central was the hard reality of the individual; institutions were penumbral.

Burke, above any other single thinker, changed this whole individualistic perspective. His *Reflections,* by its denunciations of both

19

Revolutionaries and the line of natural rights theorists leading up to the Revolutionaries, played a key role in the momentous change of perspectives involved in the passage from eighteenth-century to nineteenth-century Europe. Within a generation after publication of *Reflections* a whole *Aufklärung* blazed up in the West, at its core nothing more than an anti-Enlightenment. Such voices as Bonald, de Maistre and Chateaubriand in France, Coleridge and Southey in England, Haller, Savigny and Hegel in Germanic thought, and Donoso y Cortes and Balmes in Spain were resonating throughout the West. In America, John Adams, Alexander Hamilton and Randolph of Roanoke issued their own warnings and proposals. And all voices, European and American, were rich in respect to Edmund Burke as prophet.

To understand an effect upon the Western mind as immediate as Burke's *Reflections* was, we must take careful note of the substantial vein of a traditionalism of principle as well as emotion that had been growing up in Western Europe throughout the eighteenth century. Given our normal predilection for the more exciting Enlightenment mentality of the Voltaires, Diderots and d'Holbachs, it is easy to miss, in the histories, this counter-force to the high rationalism and individualism of the Enlightenment. But it is there all the same, a product at one and the same time of the *Church* and its still considerable numbers of philosophers and theologians committed to orthodoxy instead of the ideas of natural religion and natural ethics which had sprung out of the natural law movement of the seventeenth century. The more that the *philosophes* declared the enlightenment of their doctrines of natural rights, the more the philosophers and historians in the universities—all religiously oriented, of course—appealed to the traditions which had sustained Europe for more than a thousand years.

In addition to the church, there were the historic towns and guilds throughout Western Europe which turned increasingly, as the cosmopolitanism of the Enlightenment spread, to their own native histories, traditions, saints, heroes, governments and crafts. There were poets, composers, performers, artists, artisans, analysts and chroniclers quite content to work with the materials of their own communities instead of going off to Europe's capitals for possible fortune and fame. Search for native dialects, folk literature, long ignored creators in the arts, military heroes of the distant past, and others comparable to these, was in full swing in many parts of Germany by the middle of the eighteenth century. The fascination with the Middle Ages that would grip so many minds in England and France in the nineteenth century was widely evident in Germany and Eastern Europe throughout the eighteenth century. There was no single city in Germany that could exert intellectual power over a whole nation of the sort that both Paris and London did in their countries. Traditionalism was almost inevitable in the spirit of localism that gripped Germany and also, not to be ignored, in parts of England and France.

Long before the Revolution in France, Burke, in his *Annual Register*—book reviews which he wrote himself—and speeches had made clear his distaste for the typical rationalist mind of the French Enlightenment, and for none more than Rousseau whose talent Burke recognized but whose morals and politics he found repugnant in the extreme. He detested the Grub Street mentality in London, Paris and every place else, including New York and Boston, where it was found. From the beginning of his career in England Burke was on the side of what he saw as Britain's 'Great Tradition' in political history.

There was thus background, in Burke himself, and in England and in all Western Europe, for the kind of philosophy he set forth forthrightly in his *Reflections.* Few if any in Europe could equal Burke's eloquence of assault upon the Jacobins and their legislation in France, but by 1789 there was a considerable number of Europeans whose essential conservatism of mind was deeply ravaged by the Revolution. The words *conservative* and *conservatism* applied to politics did not appear in the West until about 1830, but the substance long preceded the words.

So far as English conservative thought is concerned, there is no doubt something which Burke, a devoted Whig, owed to the Tory Party, which was older and favored by the monarchy and much of the aristocracy. And Burke was a friend of that quintessential Tory, Dr. Johnson. But what Burke wrote in a letter to Boswell perhaps clarifies his relation to Tory principles: 'I dined with your friend Dr. Johnson on Saturday at Sir Joshua's. We had a very good day, as we had not a sentence, word, syllable, letter, comma, or tittle of any of the elements that make politics.' In the general melee of post-revolutionary politics in Britain it is probable that Tories and Whigs found themselves together often on particular issues and that by the time the new Conservative Party took shape under Peel, there was mixture too of Tory and Whig tenets. But nineteenth-century British conservatism is much more the issue of Burke and his works than of any Tories. Use of 'Tory' by modern British Conservatives has been somewhat more affectation than anything really substantive.

Burke paid a heavy price at home for his call to traditionalists throughout Europe to rally themselves against the French Revolution. He was widely charged, abroad as well as at home, with inconsistency bordering upon faithlessness of principle in taking the position he did on the Revolution in France. How, it was asked repeatedly, could he have supported the colonists in America and other tyrannized peoples of the world as he had and now turn on the French seeking emancipation from monarchical despotism? Whigs in England, including his long time friend and ally Charles Fox, broke with him on the Revolution. However, this is not the place to try to settle accounts; all we can do here is summarize briefly the case Burke made for himself. He was upholding in France the same basic principles which had actuated his defenses of the Americans, Indians and Irish against the 'arbitrary power' of the British government. In each of these defenses he had made his case on behalf of the native, historical tradition of a people under assault by an alien power. There could be no rational talk about liberty for the Americans—after all, they were fundamentally an English people abroad, living under the same prescriptions and conventions which governed the British—without the premise of a sufficient autonomy for natural development of American potentialities. The same held for Ireland and India, in each case an indigenous morality under attack by a foreign one.

In France, the assault upon traditional government and morality came from a small group of Frenchmen, the Jacobins, but, Burke argued, the essential principles of the matter were no different from those obtaining in his defense of the American colonists. The issue was freedom then and it was the same now; the violation of freedom was no less due to the fact that the minority governing was of French blood. From Burke's point of view, the Jacobins were as much aggressors upon French history and tradition as the British East India Company had been upon Indian culture. France under the Jacobins was 'exactly like a country of conquest.' Moreover, 'acting as conquerors' the Jacobins used force on the French people precisely as would an 'invading army.'

In Burke's eyes the work of the Jacobins across the Channel was the very opposite of the work done by the American colonists: the work of freedom from 'arbitrary power.' Rather it was leveling in the name of equality, nihilism in the name of liberty, and power, absolute and total, in the name of the people. The American Revolution had sought freedom for actual, living human beings and their customs and habits. But the French Revolution was far less interested in the actual and the living—the peasants, bourgeoisie, clergy, nobility, etc.—than in the kind of human beings the Revolutionary leaders believed they could manufacture through education, persuasion and when necessary force and terror. Not since Reformation insurrections in the name of God, Burke thought, had a revolution occurred in Europe so monolithically consecrated to the salvation of man and to his complete spiritual remaking.

Precisely as Anabaptists had been willing to lay waste to all that interfered with their creation of the New Christian Man, so the Jacobins, Burke perceived, were willing to destroy all institutions that interfered with the making of Revolutionary Man. Burke wrote: 'All circumstances taken together, the French Revolution is the most astonishing that has hitherto happened in the world.'

Tocqueville stressed this uniqueness of the French Revolution, also specifically disavowing a significant relationship between it and the American Revolution. That revolution had been the work of men with a clear stake in society, but not the French. On this point Tocqueville agreed completely with Burke—as he did on more than a few points. The dependence of Tocquevillian analysis—in the measured language of scholarly objectivity and with no overriding suggestion of hostility—upon Burkean polemic has not yet been sufficiently appreciated, it seems to me. In theme after theme Tocqueville dilated on Burke.

Echoing Burke, Tocqueville wrote that 'In all the annals of recorded history, we find no mention of any political revolution that took this form,' that is the form of the French Revolution. Tocqueville too looked to religious outbursts of the past for nearest precedent to the French Revolution. And Tocqueville featured the activist role of political intellectuals in the French Revolution—in striking contrast to the American Revolution. 'Men of Letters,' Burke had called them; Tocqueville used the same phrase. 'Never,' wrote Tocqueville, his very irony drawn from Burke's words, 'had the entire political education [of the French people] been the work of its men of letters.'

In another important respect Tocqueville was Burke's heir; that was the trans-Gallic, the whole European implication of the French Revolution. Burke wrote in his *Reflections:* 'Many parts of Europe are in disorder. In many others there is a hollow murmuring under ground; a confused movement is felt that threatens a general earthquake in the political world.' Tocqueville specifically designated his *Old Regime and the French Revolution* as but the first in what he planned to be series of volumes on 'the European Revolution.'

Tocqueville devoted a chapter to the essentially religious nature of the French Revolution, seeing it, as Burke specifically had, more nearly in sequence with the religious uprisings, devastations and terroristic slaughters of the late Reformation than with any political revolutions, such as the English in 1688 and the American in 1776. In somewhat the same key, Tocqueville echoes Burke's repeated charges that the French Revolutionists were men of neither experience or interest in political history or, in the true sense, political reform. 'Our revolutionaries,' Tocqueville wrote in the very phrasing of Burke,

> had [a] fondness for broad generalizations, cut-and-dried legislative systems, and a pedantic symmetry; the same contempt for hard facts; the same taste for reshaping institutions on novel, ingenious, original lines; the same desire to reconstruct the entire constitution according to the rules of logic and a preconceived system instead of trying to rectify its faulty parts. The result was nothing short of disastrous; for what is a merit in the writer may well be a vice in the statesman, and the very qualities which go to make great literature can lead to catastrophic revolutions.

Even the Jacobins' language, Tocqueville continued, 'was borrowed largely from the books they read; it was cluttered up with abstract words, gaudy flowers of speech, sonorous cliches and literary turns of phrase.' Tocqueville concludes dryly: 'All they needed, in fact, to become literary men in a small way was a better knowledge of spelling.'

It must be emphasized that throughout his *Reflections* Burke was addressing himself quite as much, if not more, to English as to French and other European sympathizers with the Jacobins. Richard Price and Tom Paine spoke for most of the sympathizers in declaring the French Revolution basically of copy of the American Revolution, primarily actuated by struggle for freedom from an oppressive power. But Burke (who would be joined here also by Tocqueville) saw the

French Revolution as much more a struggle for absolute power than for freedom, the work primarily of political intellectuals who did not have, as did the leading American revolutionists, a 'stake in society,' and were in fact society's enemies.

There is some humor in the reflection that the aims Burke ascribed to the Jacobins in 1790, aims of the reconstruction of all society, of a remaking of individual consciousness, and of the installation of a totally new religion in the place of Christianity, would have seemed much more adequate and relevant to Robespierre and Saint—Just in 1793 than would have the modest, liberal aims Richard Price had given the French Revolution in the speech at Old Jewry which triggered Burke's *Reflections.*

Burke was of course right in seeing the French Revolution as unique and also as endowed with a mystique that would reach out to all Europe, even Asia and Africa in due time, and would be perhaps the single most obsessive subject in the serious thought of the whole nineteenth century in the West. Not until the Bolshevik Revolution of 1917 would the French Revolution be at last replaced as the chief preoccupation of revolutionists everywhere and also of traditionalists and conservatives everywhere. The French Revolution is, though, the more original in its language and symbolism. In its declarations, manifestoes, and preambles to laws, in its great rolling strophes and sharp, evocative images, printed by the Jacobins to reach and fit every public square in France, the French Revolution inaugurated a kind of revolution of the Word, something previously found only in evangelical, proselytizing religions. As the history of nineteenth-century Europe reveals in almost every quarter, the Jacobin Good News, suitably translated and tactically adapted, could be the equal in force of the Christian. Marxian rhetoric, and the rhetoric of Lenin and Trotsky in 1917, was secondary, in considerable measure derivative indeed.

Burke declared Rousseau to be the chief author of the French Revolution. Tocqueville, more diffident, exonerated Rousseau, by placing responsibility upon the 'men of letters' who had, in the decade or so leading up to the Revolution, driven into the minds of the people, irresistible fantasies of freedom, equality and absolute justice. But there can be no question of Tocqueville's full awareness of Rousseau's significance. Who else, after all, had argued with such passion and eloquence the case for the people, the divinely constituted people once their chains were struck off, the iniquity of all historically formed institutions, and the absolute necessity of a 'Legislator' who would in the name of the people strike deeply and widely into human consciousness? Burke was blunt: 'I am certain that the writings of Rousseau lead directly to this kind of shameful evil.' What we know for a fact is that such Jacobins as Robespierre and Saint-Just, at the height of the Revolution, read Rousseau devotedly and regularly. Their zeal was shared, we learn from a contemporary, by a considerable number of French citizens who could be seen standing in knots at street corners reading aloud and discussing passages from the *Social Contract*, until now the least read of Rousseau's books.

Traditional groups—gilds, monasteries, corporations of all kinds —had been condemned by Rousseau, in the interest of achieving a pure general will and also the individual's own autonomy. They therefore required obliteration or substantial subordination to the nation. Aristocracy was of course marked early for extinction. But this was only the beginning. In 1791 all gilds were abolished—a goal, it is amusing to recall, that had escaped all efforts by divine-right, 'absolute' monarchies of modern France. 'There is no longer any corporation within the state,' the Law Le Chapelier read; 'there is but the particular interest of each individual and the general interest.'

Inevitably the patriarchal family felt the power of the Revolution. The general belief of *philosophes* had been that the traditional kinship structure was 'against nature and contrary to reason.' Clearly, many Jacobin governors agreed. In 1792 marriage was declared a civil contract, and a number of grounds for divorce were made available (in 1794 the number of divorces exceeded the number of marriages). Strict limitations were placed upon the paternal authority, among them the disappearance of this authority when the sons reached their legal majority. The traditional laws of primogeniture and entail were set aside forever, with implication to property as well as family.

Property was made a special object of legislative action. The over-riding aim was destruction of all linkage between property claim and the corporate organizations such as family, church, gild, and monastery which had been so long the real repositories of a very large amount of property in France—and indeed in most of Europe.

With this aim went the objective of individualizing as far as possible the rights of ownership, a part of the larger aim of individualizing all of traditional society. Moreover, the mission of exterminating the aristocracy for its parasitism involved necessarily the appropriation or the atomization of the great landed estates of the aristocracy. More fluid, mobile, and moneyed types of property flourished as one of the by products of the Revolution, elevating to economic power a whole new class. Few things would be more vividly repugnant to the conservative tradition than the Revolution's relationship to property.

There is no space here for anything approaching full recital of the varied impacts of the Revolutionary government upon traditional French society. In general, the efforts of the National Assembly, the National Convention, and the Committee on Public Safety were bent toward, at one and the same time, the *individualization* of society and the *rationalization* of everything from coinage and weights and measures to property, education, religion, and all aspects of government. Religion has perhaps claim here as one final instance of revolutionary thoroughness. At different times the government terminated all monastic and other religious vows, nationalized the Church, put all clerics on state salaries, with the binding condition that an oath of allegiance to the Revolution be taken, and then in 1793 the thrilling plan to deChristianize France completely, piously filling the vacuum with a new religion dedicated to reason and virtue. In the interest of the new religion and also of the minds of men, elaborate rituals were written, liturgies were developed for use in meetings of the new religion, and a totally new calendar was introduced for the remaking of these minds. Control of time, of the past and its images, is vital, as Orwell emphasized in *Nineteen Eighty-Four*. The French Revolutionists were ahead of him, and the proposed new calendar would have adorned a new history of the past, repudiating and destroying the mythic or tyrannical personages long celebrated and replacing them with heroes of the Jacobins' liking. The Committee on Public Safety expressed it perfectly: 'You must entirely refashion a people whom you wish to make free, to destroy its prejudices, alter its habits, limit its necessities, root up its vices, purify its desires.' Robert Palmer has written: 'In 1792 the Revolution became a thing in itself, an uncontrollable force that might eventually spend itself but which no one could direct and guide.' And Robespierre, quoted by Palmer:

'If the basis of popular government in time of peace is virtue, the basis of popular government in time of revolution is virtue and terror: virtue without terror is powerless; terror without virtue is murder.'

It was the terror that shocked Europe most about the Revolution. But Burke was one of those who without diminishing the terror saw it as less insidious than a great deal of the legislation passed by Revolutionary assemblies. The true total and boundless character of the Revolution was best observed, Burke thought, in laws designed to obliterate or seriously cripple the traditional social order and at the same time to fill whatever vacuum might be left with new arms of the state.

Even more deadly, Burke argued, was the manifest wish of the Jacobin leaders to extend the work of the Revolution to all Europe, eventually to the world. Hence Burke's ardent and repeated plea for a 'counter-revolution' to be launched by the European powers immediately. He wrote: 'If I conceive rightly, it is not a war with France but with Jacobinism. We are at war with a principle ... there is no shutting out by fortresses.'

This was precisely the attitude that conservatives would take in 1917 when the Bolsheviks overthrew the Czarist government in Russia. Leninism replaced Jacobinism.

Another revolution of the time aroused Europe's conservatives and also its romantics. I refer to the industrial revolution and its visitation upon first Europe, then the world of the steam engine, the spinning jenny, and in quick sequence a host of mechanical monsters emitting a devil's symphony of sound—and sights and odors— never before known on England's meadows and hills. There are some accounts to suggest that in the beginning at least the public took rather readily to the sight of these new mills operating in defiance of the rhythms of day and night, of the seasons, and of wet and dry, hot and cold. Perhaps they suggested release at last from man's long subjection to brute labor. If so, there would be many, often harsh, experiences ahead in the ever-proliferating factories of England to throw shadow on early suppositions.

From the beginning a large number of artists and writers opposed what they saw as the mechanization and the proletarianization of England. 'This faith in Mechanism,' wrote Carlyle, 'in the all-importance of physical things, is in every age the common refuge of Weakness and blind Discontent.' In his *Past and Present,* there is put before us, and not for the first or last time, a studied contrast between the medieval community and its vision of order and the spreading disorganization which Carlyle saw as the disease of modernity. Coleridge, Southey and Blake are but three of many who detested what Blake called 'dark, satanic mills' and Coleridge 'the catechism of Commerce.'

There was indeed a sufficient, material change in England to justify such reaction. Scarcely a stratum or sphere of institutional life was left untouched by the combined mechanical and economic revolution. Manufacturing up to this time had been very largely carried on in the homes of the workers, thus offering at least the possibility of being combined with the household economy. But now, in the new factories, workers went as individuals in the aggregate and, once there, were expected to be responsive to no ties other than the ones imposed by the manufacturing process.

Inevitably the demographic composition of England changed. Areas once of low population density because of the marginal fertility of the soil now often swarmed with people—workers were drawn by the jobs offered by factories, which were often made possible by nearby deposits of coal. Whatever rough proportion there had been between land and habitation changed radically as the new imperatives of production took over.

A new form and intensity of individualism materialized, one in which both fall and rise were possible in the social scale: the former in the move from village to slum; the latter in the opportunities offered in factories, that is the rise from worker to one or other grade of supervisor, or even manager. The effect upon the traditional status system could be profound, with a group of manufacturers, factory bosses, traders, contractors and auxiliary professionals suddenly loosed upon a society previously rooted in the far simpler gradations of rural society. New tastes and new ambitions were electric in their effects upon middle class society, heretofore rather monotonous and colorless in aspect. Ostrogorski's account of 'the breakup of the old society' is perhaps a little dramatic, but it remains, even after three quarters of a century, illuminating:

> Members of the new aristocracy of capital, whose wealth rivaled and often surpassed that of the old aristocracy of race, were anxious to mingle with the latter. At the close of the Napoleonic war, in which immense fortunes were made, a great struggle took place;

several of the new men managed to force their way into "society" and its ranks were thrown into confusion. It was in vain that society endeavored to entrench itself behind the barriers of aristocratic exclusiveness.

'In vain' is too strong; a rather formidable structure of aristocracy made its way into the twentieth century where, to be sure, it faced still other, and much more serious, challenges to its right to continue in the modern era. But we must not quibble here. As the great furor over the Reform Bill of 1832 made evident, the aristocracy, under the fierce pressures of demographic change, and the radical resettling and unsettling of ancient boroughs, lost a great deal of its monopoly of parliamentary representation. Many of the political reforms which followed that of 1832, continued its work of restructuring the voters. The ties between government and church were loosened; dissenters were granted novel political rights, as were, in time, Catholics, and although such changes are more directly the consequence of democratic forces springing from a new political spirit in the land, it was unquestionably the industrial solvent that started the dissolution of the older bonds among people. Not least among the social changes was the replacement in ever widening areas of the 'great unpaid;' that is the class of property-holders who combined affluence with performance of certain duties as unpaid magistrates in the villages and towns, by a new class of either elected or appointed civil servants. Nowhere was this particular change more quickly and lastingly felt that in the administration of the Poor Law. Henceforth administrative boards, with complete political identities, would do more or less professionally what had been done so long by landlords. Again it is useful to quote Ostrogorski:

In more than one way then man was once more caught up in the toils; another hierarchy, and with it a new species of subordination, arose in the industrial world. But the new ties, being of a purely mechanical kind, and having none of the binding force which held the old society together, not only did not check the movement but accelerated it.

Conservative reaction to industrial changes in England and then on the continent was immediate, and we learn almost as much about the conservative ideology from its efforts to cope with economic as with political change. Disraeli, in his novels especially but by no means exclusively, said much about what he perceived as a social affliction or plague, with human relationships the victims. He thought about the King in Great Britain exactly what his model, Burke, had thought about the King in France: that as sovereign he had become separated from his people by liberal reform, changes which boomeranged. 'I see no other remedy,' Disraeli declared, 'for that war of classes and creeds which now agitates and menaces us but in an earnest return to a system which may be described as one of loyalty and reverence, of popular rights and social sympathies.' In a word feudalism—the constant standard, as we shall see, of almost all changes brought about by the great political and economic changes of the century. Under the influence of romanticism, in large degree that of Walter Scott's novels, and of deeply rooted revulsion against the kinds of political and legal change which Bentham and his followers were bringing about on behalf of strictest possible modernism, a somewhat preposterous, short-lived, and in due time much satirized flurry of attention by some of the children of the greater and wealthier aristocratic households was to be seen among the ranks of the poor and needy. Largesse, 'pilgrimages of charity,' and even the introduction of cricket in the villages testified to sentimentality and romanticist escape for a short time, and then it was all gone; to be left to Disraeli and other novelists to memorialize after a fashion.

But one point must be stressed here, and will be again in the next chapter. No amount of discomfort or distress, or of offended esthetic sensibility, ever caused the conservatives to soften for a moment their tenacious regard for property—along with rank in polity their most obsessive and durable heritage.

Two other great movements in the century aroused conservative apprehension; the first religious, the second philosophical. The first was the work of the great John Wesley: Wesleyanism as it was first called, Methodism as it would be shortly known. In this latest outburst of Europe's Reformation lay a danger, most conservatives thought, to the established Anglican church in Britain and also, hardly less, to the public weal and the social structure. It is often said that the Wesleyans were a salutary force in late eighteenth- and early nineteenth-century England, in that through the appeal of their non-revolutionary gospel to the working classes, revolution was avoided by these classes. But quite apart from whatever truth may lie in that observation, it would be an oversight to declare the Wesleyans free altogether of revolutionary impulse and impact, religious rather than political the motive may have been. The revolutionary potential that had existed earlier in the Puritan forces in England was almost equally present in the minds of a great many Wesleyans.

Wesley saw his movement as in direct succession, as a revival indeed, of the Puritan temper. He too looked out and saw a church made corrupt by its formalism and disregard of the purity of faith; and beyond the established church a whole social organization that had become alienated from genuine Christian ideals and aspirations. That its motive and also movement were spiritual, not political, at the core in no way lessened the impact of Wesleyanism upon family, parish, and civil order. When the religious come to believe that the same principles which they espouse in their private, spiritual and moral lives must obtain as far as possible in the lives of all citizens, something very akin to revolution is in the making. As I have noted, the Jacobins believed that their work was in a direct line from that of the Puritans earlier in England, at the time of the Civil War.

Burke, who was Anglican and a firm believer in religious establishment, defended the civil rights of Dissenters, but he did not like them or agree with their religious tenets. How could he, given his commitment to the established Church and to an ordered realm generally? The Dissenters in Scotland, Wales, and England invariably included violence-prone members at any given time, only too eager to humiliate and harass the lives of Anglican clergy and to preach constantly its iniquity, second only to that of the Romanists.

The Wesleyans were far more contained for the most part than had been the Puritans in the seventeenth century, freer of the antinomianism that had spread through so many of the earlier Protestant sects, but despite John and Charles Wesley's best efforts, the latent enthusiasm of Wesleyanism frequently burst its banks, spilling over into the social and civil areas of English life. When a sect believes itself possessed of the absolute truth and the established church a citadel of superstition and immorality, it contains the germs of revolution. There is always threat to morality and civil law when such a sect declares itself in direct communion with God and responsible for the purification of politics as well as religion in the land.

In sum, a considerable amount of English conservatism, beginning with Burke and extending to such minds as Coleridge, Newman, Disraeli and Matthew Arnold, was activated and shaped by the religious revolution that lay in Wesleyanism and that paralleled the democratic and industrial revolutions. As is the case with most established, or otherwise routinized and conventionalized religions, Anglicanism was not given to carrying religion into the market place more often than absolutely necessary and was also prone to believe that sufficient due to God was being rendered through ritual and liturgy. Such belief is, however, like a red flag to true believers in religion.

One final irritant to the vast majority of conservatives in England was the utilitarian philosophy of Jeremy Bentham. Very little in the turbulent intellectual scene of the late eighteenth and the nineteenth centuries aroused more spleen in the Newmans and Disraelis of the time than did utilitarianism. Bentham, one of the most powerful minds in all history, had become, in his rejection of the Enlightenment, French Revolution, and all philosophers of natural rights, a good deal more of a revolutionary mind than any of them through his theories of individual interests, of hedonism, and of the greatest good to the greatest number. From these he erected a structure of centralized, minute, and penetrating authority, to be put in effect in England and every other part of the world that was at very least the equal of what Rousseau, and then Robespierre, had dreamed of through total revolution. Bentham's unfailing response when apposite was: 'the past is of no use.' Everything good proceeded from individual reason alone; reason undergirded by man's incessant search for the pleasurable and avoidance of the painful. His 'Panopticon' principle, to be applied, he insisted, to schools, hospitals, asylums, even large factories, as well as prisons, was, as Disraeli called it, 'the unlovable issue of a marriage between reason and inhumanity.' Reason alone, supplemented by knowledge of the 'felicific calculus' by which all men everywhere live, made it possible, Bentham declared, for him to legislate for all India without ever leaving his study. We can respect some of the reforms which proceeded in time from men who were avowed disciples of Bentham, foremost of which was Chadwick. Their endeavour to create a professional civil service to do what 'the great unpaid' had done for so long, and so inefficiently, it could well be argued, is respectable. But what was not respectable, what was horrifying, in the judgements of conservatives, was the nightmarish world of cold reason, bureaucracy, permanent reform, bloodless charity, and total absence of emotion and feeling that Bentham foretold.

Burke, in one of his last letters, doubtless had in mind much of the above—political, economic, religious, and philosophical disturbance of the peace of Europe—when he referred somewhat enigmatically to 'the System.' He meant the spirit of Jacobinism, in England as well as Europe, but he meant a good deal more. He meant a movement at once social and intellectual, 'the great object of which is ... to root out that thing called an aristocrat or nobleman and gentleman.' As usual, Burke is being synoptic. Behind those words lies a whole philosophy of history, an anti-progressive philosophy, one that sees the recent past as one of largely unrelieved decline from greatness, specifically medieval greatness; the greatness of an un-challenged religion, of chivalry, of great institutions like the universities, guilds, manors, and monasteries, and, last but not least, of a unified, synthesizing, body of thought. In the French Revolution and in the spirit of dissent and reform in his own cherished country, in the outbursts of economic, religious and philosophical revolt against tradition, Burke saw, it would seem, a kind of diabolical conspiracy. Notwithstanding his zeal for 'Counter-revolution' and his active participation in affairs to the end, there is a certain fatalism in his view, a resignation of spirit to the overwhelming power of modernity.

> The Evil has happened; the thing is done in principle and in example; and we must await the good pleasure of a higher hand than ours for the time of its [ending] ... All I have done for some time past, and all I shall do hereafter, will only be to clear myself from having any hand, actively or passively, in this great change.

That was Burke's valedictory, not only to the changed Whig Party, once uniquely the party of aristocracy and land, now corrupted, in his view, by the spirit of reform and revolution, but also to the whole traditional order in Europe. Emile Faguet would later refer to all of the conservatives as 'prophets of the past,' and he was entirely accurate in his judgment. It was to the past, especially the medieval past, that Burke and Bonald looked for historical exemplification of the good society. In the feudal code of chivalry, in the perfection of the gentleman, and in the proper establishment of religion, Burke found the glory that the liberals and radicals of his day reserved for the future.

This turning to the past for inspiration and for models on which to base policy in the present is deeply ingrained in the conservative tradition and is sufficient reason for liberal and radical epithets of 'reactionary' and 'archaic.' Burke sparked a general conservative fire in the nineteenth century against the philosophy of progress, against the Whig interpretation of history, largely on the basis of his view that feudal England had been more civilized in its codes of chivalry, gentleman and aristocracy than was the England Burke could see emerging from revolution and reform. All the great conservatives have made plain their allegiances to the past—which has not prevented some of them from dealing both imaginatively and boldly with such present threats as totalitarianism. Churchill said: 'I like to live in the past. I don't think people are going to get much fun in the future.' He contrasted the squalor of twentieth-century war with its magnificence in the past. Clement Attlee compared Churchill's mind to a layer cake of motivations, the bottom layer feudal in thrust, the next seventeenth century, and the one just below the top, nineteenth century in character. He hated, or so he said, mechanical gadgets and technological eyesores, but all the same he invented the tank and devised the brilliant and humane Dardanelles strategy in the First World War.

Those who look to the past instead of the future have a full view, at any rate, which is more than can be said for even the most gifted purported searchers into the future. If the past produces tiresome nostalgics, these are less a plague at the present time than are 'futurists' or 'futurologists.' Properly worked, the past is, as all comparative historians from Herodotus on have said, a vast and wonderful laboratory for the study of successes and failures in the long history of man. If we have to look beyond the present, and apparently most of us do, the past is *terra firma* by comparison with anything even the most fertile imagination—armed with the most powerful of computers—can come up with out of the liberal's cherished future.

But all that aside, there is and has been from the start an affection of the conservative for the past and its motley models. John Morley correctly wrote that the early conservatives, confronted by what they regarded as the catastrophe of the French Revolution, chose to look back upon an earlier catastrophe in European history, that of the barbarian invasion of Rome, and to the principles which eventually restored order and decency. These were of course feudal principles. And it is at bottom feudal principles that Burke, Bonald, Chateaubriand, Haller, and Hegel seized upon in the early nineteenth century to meet the perceived threats of democratic power, egalitarianism, political centralization, utilitarianism, and withal modernity. Joseph de Maistre spoke surely for most conservatives when he wrote: 'We do not want a *counter*-revolution but the *opposite* of revolution.' He was, of course, referring to the type of society conservatives cherished. To build a counter-revolutionary society would be to assume in considerable measure the character of the foe—certainly its militancy. For de Maistre the 'opposite' of the revolutionary society created by the Jacobins was essentially the society that Jacobinism had struck at, not simply the *ancien regime*—that would be too narrow and constrictive a model—but rather the feudal-medieval society that had reached its height in the thirteenth century.

2

Dogmatics of Conservatism

Ideologies, like theologies, have their dogmatics: more or less coherent and persistent bodies of belief and value which have determinative influence upon at least a part of their holders' lives. Ultimately, both relate to the individual's proper place under a system of authority, divine or secular. In conformity to a tradition going back to the Renaissance in political thought, the three modern ideologies of socialism, liberalism and conservatism are commonly dealt with in the terms of individual and state; that is, the legitimate, desired, relation between individual and state.

But a more useful perspective adds to the individual-state relationship a third factor, that of the structure of groups and associations which are intermediate to the two polar entities. As we have seen, much of the social drama of the French Revolution consisted of the impacts upon intermediate society of the newly declared rights of the individual and, equally important, the newly declared rights of power of the revolutionary state. The result was of course to put in question the historic rights of such groups as church, family, guild, and social class. Much nineteenth-century jurisprudence takes for its point of departure the rights of both old and new groups against the state on the one hand and individuals on the other. At the end of the century such eminent scholars as Maitland, Figgis and Vinogradov, followed for a time by the youthful Harold Laski, put much of the history of Western Europe, from the Middle Ages on, in the perspective of the triangular relationship of state, corporate group and individual rather than the more conventional dual relationship that had come out of the natural law tradition of state and individual. Maitland wrote of the 'pulverizing and macadamizing' forces of state and individual acting upon everything that lay in between man and state.

In Germany Otto von Gierke and in France Fustel de Coulanges were among the scholars who also made the triangular relationship central. Most of Sir Henry Maine's work with comparative institutions came down essentially to the kind of problem he had made the focus of his *Ancient Law*, the struggle between the state's claimed sovereignty and the traditional authorities of patriarchal family and clan or kindred. Such reform movements in the century as pluralism, syndicalism, gild socialism and cooperatives made the problem of the rights of groups central to larger social reform.

So did the philosophy of conservatism for the most part. More than liberalism and socialism it took to its bosom the rights of church, social class, family and property against the claims of natural rights theory and of the more recent utilitarianism on the one hand and of the national, increasingly democratic state on the other. In every one of the specific areas of conservative faith which follow in this chapter, the constant premise is the right—grown out of history and social development—of the whole intermediate structure of the nation to survival against the tides of both individualism and nationalism.

Socialism, at least in its main and eventually Marxist character, has the least regard among the three ideologies for the traditional rights of intermediate groups. The socialist position on property tended to set the stage for its views on family, local community, and above all social class. How, it was asked, implicitly at least, can the new socialist man be evolved if he remains subject to the historic smaller patriotisms as well as the bourgeois state? Socialism is thus ideologically at the opposite extreme from conservatism.

Liberalism falls about half way. As the result of Tocqueville's impress on Mill, there was an indulgence in certain areas of liberal thought for groups, especially voluntary associations, that added up to a liberal pluralism. But in the main, Mill's 'one very simple principle' together with Benthamite utilitarianism kept liberalism's overriding sympathies with the individual and his rights against the state and social group alike.

History and Tradition

Basic to conservative politics is its view of the role of history. 'History' reduced to its essentials is no more than experience, and it is from conservative trust in experience over abstract, and deductive thought in matters of human relationships that its trust in history is founded. Perhaps the most celebrated remark in Burke's *Reflections* is the one in which he specifically repudiates the Enlightenment's faith in contract: not merely contract in the sense of the social contract with which Hobbes, Locke, Pufendorf, and so many other political philosophers had drawn upon it as the foundation of the state, but contract in the far more revolutionary sense in which Rousseau had used: that is, as the continuing, permanent, premise of sovereignty. Burke wrote:

> Society is indeed a contract.... It is a partnership in all science; a partnership in all art; a partnership in every virtue, and in all perfection ...it becomes a partnership not only between those who are living but between those who are living, those who are dead, and those who are to be born.

An almost equally celebrated line in Burke, also from the *Reflections*, is: 'People will not look forward to posterity who never look backward to their ancestors.' Clearly, from Burke's point of view, the present is *not* free, as so much rationalist thought had been devoted to proving, to remake the social structure as fancy or a 'spirit of innovation' might dictate. It is not true that the legitimacy of the state is dependent solely upon the tacit consent, the incessant renewal of the social contract that Rousseau called for. Legitimacy is the work of history and of traditions which go far beyond the resources of any single generation. 'To see things authentically as a conservative,' Mannheim writes, 'is to experience events in terms of an attitude derived from circumstances and situations anchored in the past.' From the point of view of Burke, de Maistre, Savigny, and other early conservatives, true history is expressed not in linear, chronological fashion but in the persistence of structures, communities, habits, and prejudices generation after generation. The true historical method is not just a constant looking back in time, much less the telling of narrative tales; it is the method of studying the present in such a way as to bring out *all* of what lies in the present; and that means a veritable infinity of ways of behavior and of thinking which cannot be understood fully save by recognition of their anchoring in the past.

The *concreteness* of experience and history is a persisting conservative emphasis, to be seen in Burke, in Ranke, and a succession that comes down to Oakeshott and Voegelin in our day. In the Enlightenment the characteristic 'history' employed by the *philosophes,* and also a number of English rationalists, was the self-styled 'natural,' 'conjectural,' 'hypothetical' or 'reasoned' history by which one or other point was made about the present. These were by design highly abstract, and not really histories at all in the sense either of a contemporary work like Gibbon's *Decline and Fall of the Roman Empire* or Robertson's *History of Scotland* or of the historiography that would flourish everywhere in the West in the next century. What Rousseau did in his 'hypothetical' history of inequality has to be seen more as forerunner to the social evolutionary schemes of the nineteenth century than as works of history in the strict sense. When Rousseau wrote 'Let us begin by laying the facts aside, as they do not affect the question,' he was not expunging all facts; merely those irrelevant or inconsequential to his effort to demonstrate the iniquity of inequality and the means by which it achieved ascendancy in modern society. 'The investigations we enter into here' wrote Rousseau, 'must not be considered as historical truths, but only as conditional and hypothetical reasonings'—more like the hypotheses of physicists than the chronicles and annals of historians.

Adam Smith, Hume, Ferguson, Helvetius and Condorcet all wrote 'histories' of the kind Rousseau did in his Second Discourse. Adam Smith's *Wealth of Nations* was at bottom as his friend and biographer Dugald Stewart wrote, a form of history 'to illustrate the provisions made by nature in the principles of the human mind ...for a gradual and progressive augmentation in the means of national wealth.' *Natural history* was perhaps the commonest of the labels applied to this form of writing, and the phrase covered works on language, social class, mathematics, wealth, and almost every other element of civilization. Hutton wrote a 'natural history' of the universe and the earth just as Hume wrote a 'natural history' of religion.

But for Burke and the other conservatives this kind of history was worse than useless as the means of understanding the true complexity and concreteness of past and present; it was also a means, quite as abstract and deductive as the social contract theory, of bringing about reckless changes in the present without scrutiny of the details of what was being changed. There is moreover the fact, as Haller stressed, that whereas the progressive-rationalists see the present as the beginning of the future, the true way—the conservative way—is to see it as the latest point reached by the past in a continuous, seamless growth. Society is not a mechanical thing, not a machine the parts of which are both interchangeable and individually separable.

It is organic in its articulation of institutions and interrelationship of functions; also in its necessarily, irreversibly cumulative development over time.

From the conservative point of view social reality was best understood through a historical approach. We cannot know where we are, much less where we are going, until we know where we have been. This is the bedrock positions of the conservative philosophy of history. When Newman decided to respond to modernist critics, he presented his case historically, in his *Development of Christian Doctrine,* showing how current Catholic theology is a historical emergent of a past that goes all the way back to apostolic Christianity. If the past was vital, then it must be searched meticulously and objectively. Thus Ranke's famous adjuration to all historians to recover the past *wie es eigentlich gewesen ist*—exactly as it uniquely and actually happened. Ranke was criticizing, in this apothegm, not only romantic and subjective treatments of the past but also, and even more sharply, the 'natural histories' of the eighteenth century and the 'progressive developmentalism' of such pre-sociologists as Saint-Simon and Comte.

The historical method was, for conservatives, a means too of hitting back at the pestiferous utilitarians, starting with Bentham. Disraeli wrote: 'Nations have characters, and national character is precisely the quality which the new sect of statemen in their schemes and speculations either deny or overlook.' The view of the state set forth by Austin, an abstract, rationalistic, deductive view, was rejected utterly by conservative historians, beginning with Maine. To most conservatives in the nineteenth century, the repugnant effect of utilitarianism was to perpetuate the 'sophisters, calculators, and economists' Burke had treated with scorn in his *Reflections.* Such words as 'soulless,' 'icy,' 'mechanical' and 'inhuman' were regularly applied by conservatives to the Benthamite vision of state and individual. To James Thompson at the end of the century, Benthamite modernity was at bottom 'The City of Dreadful Night.'

Naturally, the conservatives, in their appeal to tradition, were not endorsing each and every idea or thing handed down from the past. The philosophy of traditionalism is, like all such philosophies, selective. A salutary tradition must come from the past but it must also be desirable in itself. It is our link with the past. 'The dead still speak' wrote Bourget in France, citing his contemporary, Vogué. This was echoed by the great literary critic-historian Brunetiere and later by T. S. Eliot. In religion and law the root word *tradere* meant handing down a 'sacred deposit.'

Some words spoken by Falkland, perhaps the truest hero of the English Civil War, are pertinent: 'When it is not *necessary* to change, it is necessary *not* to change.' Or in homelier phrasing: 'if it aint broke, don't fix it.' It is not, however, change as such that conservatives from Burke on have tended to oppose. There is no reason to doubt Burke's sincerity in the well known words: 'A state without the means of some change is without the means of its conservation.' We know he virtually adored the Revolution of 1688; and his sympathy for the American colonists rested in great part on their record of the development of English tradition.

What Burke and his successors have fought is what he called 'the spirit of innovation;' that is, the idle worship of change for its own sake; the shallow but pervasive need on the part of the masses for diversion and titillation through endless novelties. Particularly lethal is the spirit of innovation when it is applied to human institutions.

Burke's view that the real constitution of a people lies in the history of its institutions, not in a piece of paper, has been steadily echoed by conservatives to the present day. De Maistre thought the Jacobins' 'constitutions' a bad joke. They are, he wrote, 'made for Man. But there is on earth no man as such. I have seen ...Frenchmen, Italians, Russians, etc. Thanks to Montesquieu I even know that one can be Persian, but I declare that never in my life have I seen a *man*—unless indeed he exists unknown to me.' De Maistre wrote about the American constitution and, in no spirit of inconsistency, praised it and thought it boded well. But, and this is the crux, the *real* constitution in America was, and would continue to be, not the paper document but the whole constellation of customs and traditions which had formed during the two centuries of the Americans' existence in the new world. There was, he thought, admirable correspondence between what the paper constitution said, and did *not* say, and the traditions which Englishmen had brought with them to settle the glorious *New* England of Massachusetts and adjacent areas. Burke's idea of the true constitution of a people, any people, would become one of the most powerful of ideas in the nineteenth century: embodied in the multitude of English, French and German studies of constitutions and, interestingly, in the convictions of Russians like Dostovesky who came to believe so deeply in a historic, unalterable and sacred 'constitution' that was inseparable from Russia, that a lasting animadversion to Western values was built up that remains to this day.

De Maistre was amused and scornful at the idea of the Americans forsaking already built cities like New York and Philadelphia to go down to the swamp and wilderness of a piece of Maryland in order to construct *ex nihilo* the very *capital* of the new nation. It would never last, said de Maistre. But before rushing too quickly to jeer at de Maistre the prophet, it is not amiss to cheer de Maistre the traditionalist-sociologist. The by-turns pathetic and grandiose history of Washington D.C., its unending struggle for identity, and its lifelong sense of inferiority as a city compared with New York, London and Paris is fair tribute to Burke and de Maistre and their theories of constitutions and capitals.

There is another attribute of conservative veneration of the old and traditional: belief that no matter how obsolete a given structure or *modus vivendi* may be, there may be in it a continuing, still vital, *function* that man profits from, psychologically or sociologically. Surely much of the deeper thinking of Conservatives toward Liberal reform bills in the nineteenth and twentieth centuries reflected this belief. For all the *apparent* archaism and also corruption of the 'rotten boroughs' and the seemingly impotent House of Lords after its real powers had been taken away by the Liberals, was it not *possible* that these entities still performed a valuable function to society, to the social bond, and to what Burke had in mind when he wrote: 'The nature of man is intricate, the objects of society are of the greatest possible complexity, and therefore no simple disposition or direction of power can be suitable either to man's nature or to the quality of his affairs?'

History for the conservative has been very much the kind of force that natural selection is for the biological evolutionist. No individual has ever lived, or could possibly be, says the evolutionist, with the powers of decision which could bring into being the species. It is the operation of processes of selection through chance, through repeated trial and error, which alone makes possible the splendor of the biological world. There is ingrained in evolutionary selection a wisdom astronomically superior to any wisdom imaginable in a man. Efforts of breeders to do more than work *with* these natural processes of change and development are manifestly farcical.

But are not the efforts of men to do more than work with the comparable processes in human history equally farcical? Was it not at bottom farcical and also tragic for men to seek to build a new society and new human nature in France in 1789 and Russia in 1917? Such is the conservative theory of history.

John Morley somewhere likened the conservative's philosophy of life to a pale hope that things might well be better, weakly shivering alongside a gigantic conviction that things might well be a great deal worse. There is something in that of course. But in truth not very much. One does not think of the great conservatives – Burke, Disraeli, Churchill and de Gaulle – weakly shivering before anything, physical or mental. Nor do we think of Max Planck, who made one of the two or three greatest and boldest of modern discoveries in physics, shivering before the new and uncertain, though he worshipped the past and insisted that his theory had emerged from and been found in, both the old and traditional and the current in physical thought. T. S. Eliot in his essay on individual talent and tradition has written as confirmed traditionalist as well as revolutionist in poetic form and imagery. The individual talent is simply impotent, condemned to spinning of wheels, without a chosen tradition to work with.

Prejudice and Reason

One of the more audacious of Burke's attacks on the Revolution lies in his notable treatment of prejudice in *Reflections:*

> I am bold enough to confess that in this enlightened age we are generally men of untaught feelings; that instead of casting away all our old prejudices we cherish them to a very considerable degree...and the more generally they have prevailed, the more we cherish them.

For Burke, 'prejudice' is a distillation of a whole way of knowing, of understanding, and of feeling; a way he saw as being in total contrast to the ways of thought which flourished in the French Enlightenment and then, momentously, in the Revolution. Those ways put a premium on pure reason, on strict deduction of the kind found in geometry, and held up the light of *individual* truth-seeking against what was inscribed in tradition and experience. To the Revolutionists it was enough to declare a thing 'against nature and contrary to reason' to banish it forever from the polity.

But, Burke countered, much as Vico had a century earlier, the geometric way of reasoning has but the most limited of uses in human affairs. Human beings require for their nurture and advancement a different kind of reasoning, one that comes from feelings, emotions, and long experience as well as pure logic. Prejudice has its own intrinsic wisdom, one that is anterior to intellect. Prejudice 'is of ready application in the emergency; it previously engages the mind in a steady course of wisdom and virtue and does not leave the man hesitating in the moment of decision, skeptical, puzzled, and unresolved.'

For Burke prejudice is an epitomization, in the individual mind, of the authority and wisdom which lie in tradition. This was the kind of wisdom that the natural law philosophers and especially the *philosophes* took delight in exposing as mere superstition. 'With them,' wrote Burke, 'it is a sufficient motive to destroy an old scheme of things because it is an old one. As to the new, they are in no sort of fear with regard to the duration of a building run up in haste; because duration is no object to those who think little or nothing has been done before their time.' Clearly what Burke is challenging is a type of thinking that burst into prominence with the Italian humanists in the fifteenth century, that emerged again with the *philosophes,* and that would be closely associated with the intellectual mind throughout the nineteenth and twentieth centuries; to be seen in Burke's despised 'sophisters, calculators, and economists,' ever engaged in trying to think for all society and all government without stirring from their chairs.

Burke's assault upon pure rationalism through laudation of the unconscious, the pre-rational, and the traditional, found support in a great deal of nineteenth-century thought. Ironically, the Burkean idea of prejudice fed the gathering democratic idea of the will of the people, for Burke's idea was a reference above all to the kind of sense, understanding and knowledge that is *common* among individuals in a nation, not something that is the special preserve of an intellectual elite. Burke's 'prejudice' was designed to counter gnosticism, the disease of Western intellectuality that Burke's twentieth-century successor Eric Voegelin devoted a long life to tracking down from primitive Christianity to Renaissance humanists, Enlightenment rationalists, and, in our own time, Marxian socialists and Freudians. The very idea of a *gnosis* and of an intellectual elite alone qualified to express and interpret it, was repugnant to Burke. In that respect alone, there is doubtless an affinity between him and Rousseau, author of the General Will. But there is a difference. The General Will, for Rousseau, was the collective will *after* it had been purged of the traditional and purely experiential. For Burke any true 'general will' had to be of a growth of the traditional in popular consciousness.

Not many after Burke used 'prejudice,' but on its basis a durable legacy was formed, one that completed the rout of the superficial rationalism begun by the natural rights thinkers of the Enlightenment and brought to utilitarian shape by Bentham and his followers. The ever-growing interest we find in the nineteenth century in the pre-rational, in the sources of motivation and judgement which lie either outside the individual mind or else at depths within the mind which were simply unknown to Voltaire and Diderot, and, not least, in the whole sphere of folk or popular sense and sentiment, can be traced back to currents set in motion by the first conservatives.

Tocqueville clearly was proceeding from Burke's use of 'prejudice' when he wrote: 'If everyone undertook to form all his own opinions and to seek for truth by isolated paths struck out by himself alone, it would follow that no considerable number of men would ever unite in any common belief.' Newman, in his *Grammar of Assent*, meant in his 'Ilative sense,' with its explicit inclusion of the 'good sense' and 'common sense,' precisely what Burke had meant by 'prejudice.' It was also Newman who observed that men will die for a dogma who will not even stir for a conclusion. And later Chesterton warned that the merely rational soldier will not fight and the rational lover will not marry. Early in the century Disraeli had declared his war on those statesmen who seek 'to form political institutions on abstract principles of theoretic science, instead of permitting them to spring from the course of events.'

At stake in the conservative appeal to prejudice in human behavior is a whole type of knowledge. It is the kind of knowledge that William James described as 'knowledge of' in contrast to 'knowledge about.' The first is the knowledge we acquire simply through experience, through direct exposure to life or at least major areas of life. Its essence is practicality. It becomes an integral part of our characters because its origin lies in the process of habituation, of converting to generalized pre-disposition or 'instinct' the knowledge gained through experiment, conscious or unconscious, and ordinary trial and error. The second type of knowledge James adduced is that we acquire from the textbook, from learning *about* something that can be presented in the form of abstract or general principle, something that is susceptible to prescriptive formulae, and is at its most resplendent when it can be set forth in logical fashion. If immediacy and practicality are the crowning virtues of the first type of knowledge, abstractness and generality are of the second type. Knowledge *about* music or painting can be had by anyone through study. But the knowledge *of* music or art requires, in James' sense, the kind of personal experience that only musicians and painters or sculptors have and can have. Any lively imagination can come up with asserted principles or laws of government, but only someone rich in knowledge *of* can provide the practical means of leading or otherwise participating in some actual government.

This is the distinction between types of knowledge that lies behind conservative criticism of all political utopianism and a great deal of political reform. The utopian and the reformer are all too likely, argues the conservative, to be long on principle and ideal but grievously short on sense of expediency, on practicality, and the 'know how' that we expect in every artisan, from longshoreman to surgeon. From habitual devotion to rules, principles and abstractions, there is an inevitable tendency to deal with masses of people rather than with people as we actually find them as concrete individuals, as parents, communicants, workers, consumers and voters.

Michael Oakesott has put the matter nicely in a notable essay on 'rationalism in politics.' Oakeshott makes essentially the same distinction between types of knowledge that James did, using the words 'knowledge of technique' for the one and 'practical knowledge' for the other. The first is what may be acquired through intelligence, through the book or classroom, and skill in ratiocination. It is large in rules, prescriptions and generalizations. The second is strictly limited to experience, to the doing of something, and to the making of what is learned an inalienable part of one's very mind and personality. Oakeshott argues that what we call political rationalism in modern Western thought is the summation and glorification of technical knowledge, of what James called knowledge about.

The modern history of Europe, Oakeshott says, is 'littered with the projects of the politics of Rationalism.' Behind every utopia, every grand generalization about the 'course of history' or 'the nature of man,' every instant constitution for a new state or association of any kind, and every sweeping reform bill there lies the politics of Rationalism, in Oakeshott's formulation. Moreover, 'Rationalism is the assertion that what I have called practical knowledge is not knowledge at all, the assertion that, properly speaking, there is no knowledge that is not technical knowledge.' Thus the source of the familiar wail in human history that governments be in the hands of engineers, technocrats and other academic specialists. Thus the large blessing that political rationalists such as the *philosophes* in the eighteenth century bestowed upon 'enlightened despots.' It was so much more convenient to impose one's rules of political behavior upon a population if one had a pliant despot to begin with. But if one did not have such a despot already made, it would not be amiss to create one if possible. For the transmission of rationalist inspiration to the people can be slow and fitful at best if we rely on ordinary processes of participation or representation. Throughout history, therefore, wherever the rationalist mind has flourished, there has been the dream of either a single great intelligence or some small class of intelligences to rule directly and comprehensively over the people conceived as a homogeneous mass, and to be rid once and for all of the kinds of government which are founded upon mere use and wont, habit, custom and tradition, and upon representative bodies, semi-public commissions and other bodies, judicial buffers, and other restraints upon pure deductive reason.

Burke was one of the first to see that the mind of the political rationalist inclines naturally toward a kind of internal imperialism: 'democratic imperialism' as Irving Babbitt puts it in his *Leadership and Democracy*. That is, given the arrogation to individual reason of capacity to rule directly over the people, it is an easy, tempting, step forward to increase what it is that this reason is ruling – from the purely political and legal to the economic, social, moral and spiritual. It was with liberal and socialist intellectual groups in mind that Babbitt wrote: "No movement illustrates more clearly than the supposedly democratic movement the way in which the will of highly organized and resolute minorities may prevail over the will of the inert and unorganized mass."

From the conservative point of view, only prejudice, in Burke's sense, can keep a citizenry united in opposition to the kind of tyranny that rationalism in government sometimes imposes upon people.

Burke had the Jacobin rationalists in mind when he wrote the following words: "It is impossible not to observe that in the spirit of this geometrical distribution and arithmetical arrangement, these pretended citizens treat France exactly like a country of conquest." That is the criticism of bureaucracy and of the bureaucratic rationalist mentality from conservatives, and indeed from time to time liberals and socialists, that has risen constantly and sharply ever since Burke directed it against the Jacobin 'geometricians.'

Burke, and conservatives generally, have seen that almost all of the will to resist that is commonly claimed to result from inner knowledge of natural rights or from inner instincts to freedom, results instead from prejudices slowly built up historically in a people's minds: prejudices about religion, property, national autonomy and long-accustomed roles in the social order. These, not abstract rights, are the motive powers in the struggles of peoples for freedom which we honor.

Authority and Power

Authority is, along with property, one of the two central concepts in conservative philosophy. This is not to displace liberty as a conservative value; after all, Burke's repeated concern in his speeches on the American colonists, and in those on the peoples of India and Ireland, was the freedom of human beings to live by their own customs and traditions. This was the unvarying basis of his indictments of Lord North, Grenville, and Lord Hasting: their use of 'coercive power' to destroy or weaken autonomy.

But it is still necessary to see the priority of order and authority in Burke's treatment of liberty. 'The only liberty I mean,' he declared in *Reflections,* 'is a liberty connected with order; that not only exists along with order and virtue, but which cannot exist at all without them.' The first requisite of a society, Burke continues, is that means exist for the restraint of men's passions. It is important that 'the inclinations of men should frequently be thwarted, their will controlled, and their passions brought into subjections.'

The fatal flaw of the natural rights school Burke thought, had been its indifference to the walls of authority represented by traditions and social codes. Rousseau and others dealt with freedom only in the light of the claims of individual and state. But this, Burke and the other conservatives argued, is to ignore the claims of other entities, those of family, religion, local community, guild, and other institutions which are all structures of authority and which all require a substantial degree of autonomy—that is, a corporate freedom—in order to perform their necessary functions. The problem of freedom, Burke insisted, is inseparable from a triangle of authority, one involving individual and state but also the groups intermediate to these two entities.

There is an inexpugnable element of feudalism in the conservative theory of authority. Almost all conservatives in the nineteenth century—Burke, Bonald, Coleridge, Hegel, and Disraeli included—were unabashed admirers of the Middle Ages. Few changes of thought were more abrupt in the century than that from the Enlightenment's hatred of the feudal to conservative love for it and for the model it provided to cope with the political and economic pressures of modernity. Otto von Gierke, later in the century, wrote of the Middle Ages in a way that nearly all conservatives would have accepted:

> From the fundamental idea of the social organism, the Middle Ages deduced a series of other ideas. In the first place, the notion of membership was developed to portray the positions filled by individual men in the various ecclesiastical and political groups ...so that the individuals who were the elements in these bodies were conceived, not as arithmetically equal units, but as members of social groups and thereby differentiated from each other.

For Burke and other conservatives, modern history could be properly seen as a sustained decline from the medieval-feudal synthesis of authority and liberty. In medieval law 'liberty' was in the first instance the right of a corporate group to its due autonomy. The whole panorama of Western history could be seen as the disintegration of this social, corporate conception into one dominated by masses of individuals. Tocqueville's underlying philosophy of history in his *Democracy in America* is one in which both the political state and the individual advance in importance at the expense of the social bonds within which both were largely confined in the Middle Ages. Authority then was manifest in a chain, one analogous to the chain of being that dominated medieval theology. Both liberty and authority were inescapable aspects of a chain of groups and associations rising from the individual to family, parish, church, state, and ultimately to God. This sense of authority as a chain or hierarchy played a major role in the conservative view of society.

Burke's view of the proper design of authority within the state is lucidly and pointedly set forth in his *Thoughts and Details on Scarcity,* written in 1795 at the request of Pitt, the then Prime Minister. Pitt had asked Burke for his recommendation of the desirable approach that government should take in the event of an internal disaster such as a severe famine. What organization of government powers should prevail? Burke's answer was crisp and to the point. Organization should remain the same, whether in normal or exceptional times:

> The State ought to confine itself to what regards the State or the creatures of the State, namely the exterior establishment of religion, its magistracy, its military force by land and sea, its revenue, the corporations that owe their existence to its fiat; in a word, everything that is truly and properly public, to the public peace, to the public safety, to the public order, and to the public property.

But *not,* Burke emphasizes, to problems and necessities of the private sphere. In this there is not the slightest distinction between Burke and his friend Adam Smith. Indeed in Smith's *Wealth of Nations,* government may legitimately take on education and certain other actions which are necessary to the public weal and which may not commend themselves to private initiative. But Burke is silent on any such additions to the government's responsibility to its citizens. Despite the occasional intimations from time to time among self-styled Burkean conservatives that Burke followed a different drummer than Adam Smith, there is in fact no serious difference between them on the function of government. It is a matter of record that Burke's admiration for Smith's *Wealth of Nations* was immense, fully as great as for Smith's earlier work, *Theory of Moral Sentiments,* which Burke had reviewed with almost extravagant praise in his *Annual Register.*

The feudal-conservative structure of political authority is also strong in Burke's *Thoughts and Details.* Burke is writing about government powers:

> As they descend from the state to a province, from a province to a parish, and from a parish to a private house, they go on accelerated in their fall. They cannot do the lower duty, and in proportion as they try it, they will certainly fail in the higher. They ought to know the different departments of things; what belongs to laws and what manners alone can regulate. To these, great politicians may give a leaning, but they cannot give a law.

Laissez-faire and decentralization are sovereign in Burke.

The essentially feudal view of authority prevailed in Germany, France, and other parts of Europe in conservative writing. Bonald's *Theory of Power,* published a year before Burke's death, and with acknowledgement of the stimulus of Burke's *Reflections,* advanced a philosophy of authority and power that might have come straight from Thomas Aquinas. Sovereignty, Bonald declared, exists in God alone. He delegates this sovereignty more or less equally between family, church and political government. Each share of this divinely distributed authority is to be regarded as supreme in its own realm. The authority—and thereby the freedom or autonomy—of the family is sacrosanct; neither the state nor the church may rightfully transgress upon the prerogatives belonging to kinship. The same precisely holds for government and church. Each has its own due and proper authority over its own. Tyranny consists, Bonald wrote, in the transgression of one sphere upon another. The total power of the Revolutionary state in France had come from its wanton invasion of the spheres of family and church.

This was a common view. In Germany, Hegel presented, in his *Philosophy of Right,* a substantially similar view. The powers of church, aristocracy, family, and political government are set forth pluralistically. The state must never transgress upon the rights and autonomies of the major social groups and strata. Haller built his entire, monumental *Theory of the Political and Social Sciences* around this pluralism, this separation of spheres, and the rights of all groups and associations beginning with the family. Again it is instructive to remember de Maistre's injunction to build a society, not merely counter-Revolution but the *opposite* of the Revolution. And this the conservatives did, beginning with Burke.

Nor have these principles of state and society ever left conservatism, save under the spurs of emergency and sheer political necessity. Disraeli, Newman, Tocqueville, Bourget, Godkin, Babbitt, all of them, down to such conservatives of our own day as Oakeshott, Voegelin, Jouvenel and Kirk, have stressed nothing if not the bounden necessity of the political state holding as far back as possible from meddling in economic, social and moral affairs; and, conversely, in *doing* all that is possible in strengthening and broadening the functions of family, neighborhood, and voluntary, cooperative association. And in practical politics over the last two centuries, in America as in European countries, the hallmark of conservative politics has been its greater affection for the private sector, for family and local community, for economy and private property, and for a substantial measure of decentralization in government, one that would respect the corporate rights of the smaller unities of state and society. However bizarre it may seem at first thought to attach the label of feudal to such American products as Coolidge, Hoover, Goldwater and Reagan—and their British counterparts—their philosophies of government earn the label all the same.

What Burke, Bonald and Hegel began in this respect remained a sturdy heritage all through the nineteenth century. Newman, in one of the few pieces on government that he ever wrote, saw proper authority in the state as based upon the four principles of *coordination, subordination, delegation* and *participation*—in that order. They are, in concert, feudal to the core. In France, the critical writings of Bourget and the novels of Barrés offer like perspectives of authority. In both we find the stress on the social bond, the relative insignificance of the individual, love of tradition, hierarchy, and heroism; and withal, as Bourget stated, 'the disposition to feudalize and decentralize everything political.'

One of the legacies of the conservative-feudal view of government and society is that of semi-public autonomous bodies in the realm, freed of direct responsibility to legislature or the people. Lord Keynes acknowledged conservative wisdom in this respect, calling for greater use of such bodies in the economic and social affairs of a nation, thus taking a load off the state and at the same time perhaps cutting off the roots of what would otherwise be endless bureaucracy. The Middle Ages had of course been rich in such groups as these, and more than a few of them remained intact in Europe for a long time after the idea of the centralized, direct state had come into circulation. Such groups as the University Grants Commission in England and the Federal Reserve in the United States are obvious instances here, though neither appears likely to remain for long, given the constant opposition of populist and direct democracy elements. Courts had had extraordinary privileges in medieval society, and they have continued in the West to have at least a degree of feudal autonomy, certainly as compared with the status of courts in the totalitarian nations. The Supreme Court—also the object of almost incessant attack by populists and social democrats—has always been in many respects the favorite branch of government in the hearts of

American conservatives. It was the voice of conservatism that made possible until early in the twentieth century the indirect election of U.S. senators. The Senate was designed by the Framers as the 'conservatives' chamber, comparable in its way to the House of Lords in Britain. Better, then, for senators to be spared campaigns directly among the voters, and to mandate their elections by state legislatures, another example of conservatism's preference for indirect government and its inevitable buffering institutions and safeguards. One will search the history of conservative thought in vain for anything resembling a 'one man, one vote' philosophy. Conservatives fought as hard in the United States for indirect elections of officials, in the local communities and the states as well as the national government as English conservatives had fought for 'rotten' boroughs and the strength of the House of Lords. The highly democratic measures of initiative, recall and referendum which came into being in the American states around the turn of the century were opposed every step of the way by conservatives—whether Democrat or Republican.

The Constitution of the United States was a very conservative piece of work when its drafters concluded their labors in Philadelphia. The conservative principles of division of powers, of checks and balances, of indirect government, and built-in limitations generally upon possible tendencies of the national government to go the way of European governments, were to be seen in almost every part of the Constitution. The liberties of individuals would be best guarded by making certain that national government could not, save in the rarest circumstances, interfere in any way with the authorities of the states and, within them, local communities. When the idea of a special bill of rights came up, Alexander Hamilton spoke for almost all conservatives in his opposition. Such a bill was unnecessary in the first place; in England, Magna Charta and later petitions of rights were appropriate and valuable simply because there was at the time little if any power of the people recognized; it had been surrendered to the monarchy. 'Here,' wrote Hamilton, 'the people surrender nothing; and as they retain everything, they have no need of particular reservations.'

The freedom of individuals and of local and regional bodies could best be protected, and combined with opportunities for their freer development and prosperity, by careful avoidance of prescription for them in the Constitution. Liberties, individual and communal, existed, as it were, in the interstices of the Constitution. Hence Hamilton's opposition to a separate bill of rights.

> Why declare that things shall not be done which there is no power to do? Why, for instance, should it be said that the liberty of the press shall not be restrained when no power is given by which restrictions may be imposed? Moreover if gratuitous mention of such a liberty were to be made in the constitution, it would in the first place threaten to elevate it above other possible liberties, no less important, but penalized by their omission from the document.

In any event, Hamilton continued, 'What signifies a declaration that the liberty of the press shall be inviolably preserved? What is the liberty of the press? Who can give it any definition which would not leave the utmost latitude for evasion?' The long and often tortured history of the First Amendment suggests that Hamilton and his fellow conservatives were not without a certain prophetic insight. At bottom, their doctrine of liberties was essentially that of medieval law: that these are best served within the doctrine of the maximum liberty for corporate bodies, such as family, domain, corporation; and served also by the principle of separation, of localization or regionalization, and of competition among powers. Over and over again constitutional history in America is one of conflict between those insisting upon maximization of *individual* rights and those insisting upon the autonomies of the *corporate* rights of states and local communities.

Let it not, though, be thought that conservatives have been or are in favor of a weak central government. Far from it. The distinction that Tocqueville made in *Democracy in America* between *government* and *administration* is implicit at least in almost all conservative thought. The former, Tocqueville wrote, must be strong and unified. It is the latter that must, in the interest of liberty and order alike, be as decentralized, localized, and generally inconspicuous as possible. De Maistre declared the public executioner the very cornerstone of proper governmental power over the people. We tend, he writes, to shrink from him: 'And yet all grandeur, all power, subordination rests on the executioner; he is the horror and the bond of human association.' De Maistre mocks the public's common praise of the soldier and its repugnance for the executioner. The soldier kills and kills; his cause changes constantly; there are never enough of him; and he is the constant threat to civil government. The executioner, however, is small in number, inconspicuous, and constant in purpose: he is there to prevent as well as punish crime. 'Since crime is part of the world's order,' wrote de Maistre, 'and since it can be checked only by punishment, once deprive the world of the executioner and all order will disappear with him.' But from centrality of government it does not follow that it must be omnicompetent, responsible for daily existence, and ever in our lives, and, worst of all, pretended moral teacher, guide to virtue, and mother of spirit.

The price, Burke warned, of the eradication or erosion of all the natural authorities in a society, is increasing military domination of the government. There is no alternative to this, he writes at the end of the *Reflections,* 'for you have industriously destroyed all the opinions and prejudices...all the instincts which support government....You lay down metaphysical propositions which infer universal consequences, and then you attempt to limit logic by despotism.' Most of the conservatives of the mainstream have put the problem of authority in these Burkean terms. Burckhardt, who loathed the kind of individualism he had found in the Italian Renaissance, in its 'rootless' humanists in war against everything traditional and communal, ever eager to serve the new money and the new power of Renaissance Italy, saw the future of the West in Burkean terms. He thought the glorification of human nature, the belief in the intrinsic goodness of individuals, a force in itself capable of destroying the social fabric, thus leaving human beings in time the helpless subjects of a new race of 'booted commandoes.'

There was no real conflict, the conservatives argued, between the needs of political government and the claims of the social and moral spheres to autonomy. 'Such divisions of our country as have been formed by habit and not by a sudden jerk of authority, were so many little images of the great country in which the heart found something it could fill. The love to the whole is not extinguished by this subordinate partiality.' Those words were written by Burke in his indictment of the French schemes of 'geometrical symmetry' in the state, of a centralization of power in the name of reason that would not only destroy all the 'inns and resting-places' and 'our neighborhoods and provincial connections' but 'confound all citizens ... into one homogeneous mass.'

What kept Burke's and Bonald's visions of state and society alive in the nineteenth century was the pervasive impact of Benthamite utilitarianism. The hatred of this philosophy that we find in the pages of Newman, Disraeli and almost all other conservative thinkers was the successor to Burke's and Bonald's earlier hatred of natural rights and natural law individualism generally. Bentham possessed a far greater brilliance of mind, and also of the Messianic, than any of the *philosophes* with the exception of Rousseau; and he was able to attract followers, many of them exemplary reformers of government, as Rousseau never could—save in so far as his nihilistic attitude toward all inequality in society furnished generalized inspiration to revolutionists and powerseekers. For Bentham the sight of pluralistic diversity, of the old and new mixed, of the purely local or regional, above all of the traditional—'sordid fingers of the past'— was enough to inspire rage. His panopticon principle, at first limited to prisons, became before his death the epitome of his icy rationalism with respect to all human arrangements—asylums, schools, factories, etc. His 'greatest good for the greatest number' was quite literally given detail through a 'felicific calculus,' and Bentham seems never to have doubted that the 'two sovereign masters' of man were desire for pleasure and recoil from pain. Social, cultural, even racial or ethnic, characteristics were, in Bentham's view, irrelevant and immaterial.

Tocqueville could have had Benthamite democracy in mind when he wrote of the kind of power over human lives that democracies have most to fear in themselves:

> an innumerable multitude of men, all equal and alike, incessantly endeavoring to procure the petty and paltry pleasures with which they glut their lives ... [above it] an immense and tutelary power ... absolute, minute, regular, provident and mild ... till each nation is reduced to nothing better than a flock of timid and industrious animals, of which the government is the shepherd.

Conservative thought has had this view of democractic despotism in the forefront of its consideration of democracy from Burke on. 'A perfect democracy,' Burke wrote, 'is the most shameless thing in the world. As it is the most shameless, it is also the most fearless.' The most fearless, that is, with respect to the social order and its inherent authorities and autonomies. Bonald wrote: 'Monarchy instinctively recognizes society and its constitutive groups, whereas democracy constantly seeks to supplant them.' Irving Babbitt in his study of democracy and leadership saw in democracy an ineradicable 'imperialism' that seeks constantly to bring the diversity of society under its own uniform, equalitarian mould.

Burke and Bonald both blamed the democratic forces of the Revolution for the vast increase in government bureaucracy. Once the state begins to substitute its own authority and distinctive pattern upon the myriad forms of society, there is no alternative to an ever-widening bureaucracy. Tocqueville went so far as to declare that so close are democracy and bureaucracy in spirit that one may predict the advance of democracy by the advance of bureaucracy, and vice versa.

So too is there a close affinity between democracy and the widening and leveling of warfare. It was the Revolution, as all the early conservatives pointed out, that instituted for the first time in history, a national conscription, the famous *levée en masse*. Warfare, all of a sudden, lost the limited character it had had in the pre-Revolutionary age, with more or less finite purposes—usually dynastic or territorial—a fixed order of battle, and a great deal of post-feudal ceremony. With the Revolutionary armies on the march, war became the crusade for freedom, equality and fraternity that inevitably brought with it the ever-larger armies and ever-expanding purposes seen in the nineteenth century. Taine observed that democracy puts a knapsack on every male while it gives him the ballot. In the twentieth century mass warfare of the kind that had engendered only forebodings before, became a reality in the First World War, with millions of men locked in a military slaughterhouse, with all the ancient art of war supplanted by huge, nearly motionless armies systematically raining shells upon one another, the prize being little more in a given battle than an advance of a few hundred yards. Winston Churchill wrote: 'War, which used to be cruel and magnificent, has now become cruel and squalid.' All, Churchill added, because of science and democracy, each a great leveller. It was the conservative Major General Fuller in England between the world wars who gave historical length and breadth to Churchill's words, showing in detail the close relation historically between the expansion of the demographic and political base of the national state and the expansion also of the whole pattern of war in the West: its mass in purely human terms, the ever-more lethal weaponry, and, especially, the widening of the aims of war from the simple territorial and dynastic to the ideological and moral. In the feudal era, as Fuller, Dawson, Churchill and other conservatives have stressed, war was limited in almost every respect: by its technology, the number of those involved, by its code of chivalry, by limited contract or obligation to serve, and by church interdictions. By contrast, at the onset of the Second World War, the democratic societies of the West had achieved limitless objectives, unconditional terms of surrender, a weaponry that could kill by the hundreds of thousands, and death and devastation greater in a single year than of all previous wars combined.

The masses represent yet another perspective of the conservative treatment of political power; the masses and their relationship to the centralization and thickening of power in the Western state. I use 'masses' here in the sense in which we find it in the writings of Ortega y Gasset and Hannah Arendt, among many others: an aggregate discernible less by numbers than its lack of internal social structure, integrating tradition, and shared moral values. One of the effects of the Revolution's peculiar form of nihilism, Burke thought, was its effective desocializing of human beings, its atomizing of the population by virtue of its destructiveness toward traditional social bonds. Thus Burke refers to the Revolution 'tearing asunder the bands of their subordinate community and [dissolving] it into an unsocial, uncivil, unconnected chaos of elementary particles.' Elsewhere he writes that the Revolutionary government has 'attempted to confound all sorts of citizens, as well as they could, into one homogeneous mass, and then they have divided this amalgam into a number of incoherent republics.'

The idea of the mass developed and spread widely in the nineteenth century. It is strong in Tocqueville, who thought one of the great dangers of democracy was its creation of the mass in the first place—through emphasis upon the majority and through egalitarian values which tended to level populations—and then its increasing dependence upon the mass, leading to plebiscitary dictatorship. Burckhardt, Nietzsche and Kierkegaard, all wrote in apprehension of the coming of mass society and its desocializing effect upon the individual; an effect that would make government a combination of guardian and despot.

There was thus a considerable tradition of the use of the 'masses' in Western thought before Ortega y Gasset brought forth his *Revolt of the Masses* in 1929. There is a close, symbiotic relation, Ortega thought, between the creation of the masses in modern life and the creation of the totalitarian state. How can the state not be total in its power and responsibility, Ortega asks, when the population it governs has become denuded of all the forms of authority and function which once made a social organization of it? In turn, though, 'the masses feel the power of the state to be theirs. Through and by means of the State, the anonymous machine, the masses act for themselves.' Peter Drucker somewhat later, and with Hitler's Germany primarily in mind, wrote that 'the despair of the masses is the key to understanding fascism.' No 'revolt of the mob,' no 'triumph of unscrupulous progaganda,' but 'stark despair caused by the breakdown of the old order and the absence of a new one.' This, Drucker concluded, in *The End of Economic Man,* is the origin and the *raison d'être* of the totalitarian state. Hannah Arendt only echoed this conservative litany on the masses in her monumental *The Origins of Totalitarianism.*

Liberty and Equality

There is no principle more basic in the conservative philosophy than that of the inherent and absolute incompatibility between liberty and equality. Such incompatibility springs from the contrary objectives of the two values. The abiding purpose of liberty is its protection of individual and family property—a word used in its widest sense to include the immaterial as well as the material in life. The inherent objective of equality, on the other hand, is that of some kind of redistribution or leveling of the unequally shared material and immaterial values of a community. Moreover, individual strengths of mind and body being different from birth, all efforts to compensate through law and government for this diversity of strengths can only cripple the liberties of those involved; especially the liberties of the strongest and the most brilliant. This is, in brief, the view which conservative writers have unfailingly taken, from Burke on, on the relation between liberty and equality.

Burke's indictment of the French Revolution and his rigorous differentiation of it from the American Revolution rested in large measure upon what he perceived as the diametrically different resolutions of liberty and equality in the two events. The earlier revolution was, Burke thought, motivated solely by the desire for freedom: freedom of the colonies from British rule and, through its constitution, freedom of the people from a government that might seek to impose its will illegitimately upon the inherent rights of individual citizens. But the French Revolution from the beginning, Burke thought, made equality and the nation the two dominant values, both possible instruments of tyranny, and correspondingly worked toward the erosion of the social and moral conditions of the liberty of citizens.

Burke saw the French Revolution, its Declaration of Rights, its successive constitutions, and a multitude of its laws, as an unprecedented and hateful effort to transfer the primary locus of freedom from the individual to the nation. The Revolutionary slogan for the nation, *une et indivisible,* left no crevices, no openings in the body politic through which energetic individuals might rise. The freedom that the Jacobins celebrated, Burke believed, was essentially the freedom of the people as a national community to act against all groups, beginning with the aristocracy and the monarchists, which sought to limit or qualify in any way this monolithic community. The highest kind of freedom was not 'freedom from' but rather 'freedom to;' in a word, to participate in some community or cause larger than one's self. This had been the essence of Rousseau's revolutionary treatment of freedom in his *Social Contract.* Everywhere, Rousseau wrote electrifyingly, man is in chains though he was born free. To strike off the chains was the objective Rousseau sent to all future revolutionists and reformers, but with this message went another, more subtle but more powerful. True freedom lies in the individual's total surrender of self and all possessions, including rights, to the absolute community. From Rousseau to Lenin, that has been the essentially collectivist—or communal—interpretation of true freedom.

The message has been the unfailing object of conservative assault. Power is power, Tocqueville said in effect: it does not matter whether the power is wielded by one man, a clique, or the whole people. It is still power and therefore oppressive. From this position, set forth from the beginning by Burke and echoed immediately by de Maistre and Bonald, rose the conservative insight into the potentially despotic nature of popular government. The seductive thought that enlargement of the base of power would be automatically to diminish use of power, since the people would not tyrannize themselves, would lead, conservatives argued, to a novel form of despotism in which the entire people, or a simple majority, might impose its tyrannical will upon minorities, creative elites, and other lesser bodies of human beings in society. A conservative mocked the Rousseauian-Jacobin view of freedom by writing: Each morning the citizen would look into the mirror while shaving and see the face of one ten-millionth a tyrant and one whole slave.

I mentioned earlier in this section the conservative fondness for the intermediate social groups and communities in the social order: those which mediate between individual and the larger political power. That was in the context of a theory of authority. Here it is important to stress the degree to which the same emphasis upon intermediate groups became the basis of a conservative view of freedom. Groups of individuals—classes, communities, guilds and corporations—seemed to Burke and Tocqueville alike to have been the principal victims of the Revolution in France: these rather than abstract individuals. Burke repeatedly referred to violations of the corporate and communal rights of Frenchmen by the Jacobins: rights in kinship, religious, economic, and other kinds of associations.

There is thus implicit in the conservative defense of groups against the sovereign a pluralism that would become one of the more distinctive philosophies of the later nineteenth century. At various times this pluralism—and also syndicalism—could be taken up by conservative, liberal, and radical causes alike—visible in Proudhonian anarchism and in the anarchism of Kropotkin later and the liberalism of Mill as well as the conservatism of Hegel, Tocqueville and Taine. The thesis common to all these causes is the very reverse of that enunciated by Rousseau and the Jacobins. The claims of intermediate groups upon their members do not add up to tyranny but to the reinforcements necessary to the liberty of individuals. If the rights of such groups as family, community and province are invaded by the central state—and almost predictably in the name of individuals assertedly robbed of their natural rights—the true walls of individual freedom will in time crumble. The conservative position, set forth most eloquently by Tocqueville, is that intermediate associations are valuable as mediating and nurturing contexts for individuals and equally valuable as buffers against the power of the state. In democracies especially, declared Tocqueville, these intermediate associations are necessary, for they offset, by their very existence and the loyalties they win from their members, the ever-mesmerizing power of the social democratic state and its creed of equality.

The conservative stress on such groups as family, church and local community is in practice a stress too upon the several social roles which exist perforce in these groups. There has been a minimum of support, consequently, from the conservative wing for the varied liberationist movements of the twentieth century. Given apprehension of the masses, of threatened break-up of social molecules into atoms, of a generalized nihilism toward society and culture as the result of individualistic hedonism and the fragmenting effect of both state and economy upon the traditional communities, it is hardly matter for surprise that conservatives have from the beginning been in the forefront of resistance to feminist movements. To cherish and respect the woman in her role of mother, wife, daughter is one thing, the conservative might be heard saying; it is something unacceptably different to see the woman being separated from her historic roles by modern liberalism. Much the same position is characteristically taken in religion, education, not to forget political citizenship itself where conservatives for long opposed voting rights (and economic too) for women on the ground that their presence on the hustings would at once defeminize them and feminize the roles and issues of politics. Probably nowhere has the innate feudalism of the conservative ethic been more visible than in the recurrent response of conservatism to the successive liberationist movements of the modern world. Where the liberal sees a probable increase in freedom and creativeness the result of these liberations, the conservative is more likely to see, or at least fear, insecurity and alienation.

The chief accusation made against liberalism by conservatives is, and has been from Burke to Dawson, Eliot and Kirk among moderns that liberalism is a kind of Judas goat for totalitarianism. By its incessant liberationist work on the traditional authorities and roles in society, liberalism, it is argued, weakens the social structure, encourages the multiplication of 'mass-types' of human beings and thus beckons in its way to waiting totalitarian masters. 'By destroying the social habits of the people,' wrote Eliot, 'by dissolving their natural collective consciousness into individual constituents....Liberalism can prepare the way for that which is its own negation.' It was during the heyday of Mussolini that Christopher Dawson pronounced Italian Fascism the work basically of modern liberalism.

Equality is no more popular in the conservative tradition than the liberal view of individual freedom. I have stressed the feudal model for a great deal of conservative thinking about society and state. Nowhere is this model more visible than in the treatments of equality, leveling, and of uniformity, the absence of vital differentiation, the mass character of which equality run rampant can bring about in a society. As we have noted, feudalism is the translation into politics of the theology of the chain of being. Inequality of function, role and power is as necessary to the social order as a whole as to the family. 'Take but degree away, untune that string, and hark! what discord follows; each thing meets in mere oppugnancy.' Thus the familiar view of Shakespeare toward the leveling of ranks.

It is the view of all conservatives. Social differentiation, hierarchy, and functional rather than mechanical consensus are as vital to freedom as to order. This is the nub of the conservative philosophy of freedom and equality. The socialist may see the latter as fundamental to the former. The liberal is more and more disposed to agree. But, save only for the kind of legal and constitutional equality which England was the first to reach, in the seventeenth century, most forms of equality—or, better, of mechanisms of achievement of equality—seem to the conservative to threaten the liberties of both individual and group, liberties which are inseparable from the built-in differentiation, variety, and variable opportunity that are so often the target of the equalizer.

'Those who attempt to level, never equalize,' Burke wrote in a famous line. He concedes readily the importance of vertical as well as horizontal channels of individual movement in a creative and productive society. 'Woe to the country which would madly and impiously reject the service of the talents and virtues' of the common people. There must be ways for individuals of lower station to rise to higher. But such rise must not be too easy. 'If rare merit be the rarest of all rare things, it ought to pass through some sort of gradation.'

In *Coningsby* Disraeli wrote to fellow Jews that equality would be particularly oppressive to them, given their history. 'Their bias is to religion, property, and natural aristocracy; and it should be the interest of statesmen that this bias of a great race should be encouraged and their energies and creative power enlisted in the cause of existing society.' Only, Disraeli suggests, when Jews are denied the privileges of citizenship and of protection of their natural aristocracy and property and religion, are some Jews forced into aberrant, radical behavior.

Much of the conservative veneration for the family lies in the historic affinity between family and property. It is usually the rule for any family to seek as much advantage for its children and other members as is possible. The medieval laws of primogeniture and entail by which family property could pass intact to the oldest son and by trust and could not be alienated from the family line obviously bespoke a high regard for the family as the best possible means of protection against dissipation and fragmentation of property, its center of gravity almost invariably land. There is no issue over which conservative has fought liberal and socialist as strenuously as on threats through law to loosen property from family grasp, by taxation or by any other form of redistribution. The argument against the hoary protections of family privilege came down to the unfair advantage one set of children would have over another by reason of differential inheritance.

But, answers the conservative, we do not protest the unequal advantage given one set of children by virtue of genetic transmission of qualities of strength and acuity; why, then, should we protest the inheritance of cultural-material qualities—which may have required several generations in the formation—which are equally a part of what we think of as family and ancestry? Hayek puts the conservative case succinctly:

> To admit this is merely to recognize that the belonging to a particular family is part of the individual personality, that society is made up as much of families as individuals, and that transmission of the heritage of civilization within the family is as important a tool in man's striving toward better things as is the heredity of beneficial physical attributes.

Further, given the presumably ineradicable desire everywhere of parents to seek as much preferment for their own children as possible, the simple transmission of property is less costly overall to a society than is—in societies such as Communist nations where inheritance of property has been forbidden—the scurrying around of parents to get their children in the best jobs, at whatever cost to the good of society. T. S. Eliot has noted that the now-familiar competition, often vicious, of parents to get their children a place in the best schools and colleges, at whatever loss to both child and curriculum, is the frenzied recourse people have to ways which may compensate for loss of older and recognized strata of position in the social order.

But Carlyle had said it earlier for conservatives. Recognized or not recognized, a man has his superiors, a regular hierarchy above him; extending up, degree above degree to heaven itself and God the Maker, who made His world not for anarchy but for rule and order. Before money—cash—had become 'the universal sole nexus of man to man,' the lower classes, Carlyle went on, had those to whom they could more or less naturally look up to. 'With the supreme triumph of Cash, a changed time has entered; there must a changed aristocracy enter.' Carlyle was not pleading for restoration of the semi-feudal aristocracy of the eighteenth century in England but rather one of mind and heart. But his outlook on the new world around him was pure, Burkean conservatism.

Conservatives recognized early the leveling, egalitarian potentialities of law—formal, statute law. As Halévy wrote: 'It may be said of all laws that they are in their essence equalitarian and individualistic insofar as they tend to consider all individuals as equal and to equalize the conditions of all individuals.' Law is in short more often the destroyer of custom than it is the creator.

Conservative opposition—almost tropistic from the very beginning—to redistribution, special entitlements, and Affirmative Action programs, springs from the inevitably devastating effects in the long run of these upon the diversity and variety of society as much, if not more, as its hierarchies. Hierarchy of one kind or other will never be wiped out by law. As efforts to this effect in the socialist societies have shown, and nowhere more grossly than in the Soviet Union, there is little if any eradication of hierarchy; only a massive shift in the bases of class-power and class-wealth. But what is wiped out, on the clear evidence, is the cultural, social, psychological and social-ecological *diversity* of a people when serious redistribution takes effect. Jouvenel has written on this in his *Ethics of Redistribution:*

I for one would see without chagrin the disappearance of many activities which serve the richer, but no one surely would gladly accept the disappearance of all the activities which find their market in the classes enjoying more than £500 of net income. The production of all first-quality goods would cease.

And the further consequences?

Firstly, personal hardship for individuals of original tastes; secondly, the loss to society of the special effort these people would make to satisfy their special needs; thirdly, the loss to society of the variety of ways resulting from successful efforts to satisfy special wants; fourthly, the loss to society of these activities which are supported by minority means.

Of all conservatives writing during the past two centuries on 'leveling,' 'homogeneity of the mass,' and the 'sterilization of rank and status' in modern democratic society, no one has yet outdone Tocqueville in the matter. In *Democracy in America* he pretended to an Olympian detachment that he did not in fact ever hold personally. His *Recollections,* the memoir he wrote on his participation in the Revolution of 1848 in Paris, makes clear his antipathy to the kind of equality that 'penetrates into the minds of the people in the shape of envious and greedy desires and sow the seed of future revolutions.' It is almost comical at times in *Democracy in America* to see the author over and over again come up with brightest countenance, so to speak, to equality and then, after perfunctory praise, lapse into the general mood of pessimism and fear that hangs over that classic, especially Part II—which should have been published as a separate book with the title *Equality.* Readers have no difficulty in finding stated in Tocqueville—often turgidly and anfractuously but with power all the same—the secular theology behind Orwell's *Animal Farm.*

Property and Life

'To the civilized man,' wrote Paul Elmer More in 1915, 'the rights of property are more important than the right to life.' After all, More goes on, life is a primitive thing; that is, no more than the biological basis of the values we cherish as civilized. 'Nearly all that makes it more significant to us than to the beast is associated with our possessions—with property, all the way from the food we share with the beasts, to the most refined products of the human imagination.'

It is interesting to know that these words were written by their author in direct excoriation of John D. Rockefeller; however, *not* of Rockefeller's role in the so-called Ludlow Massacre in Colorado, when workers were killed on Rockefeller mining property for their refusal to disperse when ordered by the police; not at all for this. More's declaration that property is more vital than life was provoked by what he felt to be Rockefeller's mealy-mouthed, uncertain and wavering *defense* of his actions in the protection of his private property.

'It is the contempt for property,' Burke wrote in a letter in 1793, 'and the setting up against its principle certain pretended advantages of the state (which by the way exists only for its conservation) that has led to all the other evils which have ruined France and brought all Europe into the most imminent danger.'

Repeatedly, in the *Reflections* and almost everything else Burke wrote about the French Revolution and the European crisis produced by the Revolution, he makes Jacobin assault upon private property, through obliteration, national appropriation or severe regulation, a crime equal to anything done to Christianity or monarchy and aristocracy. Nothing affords better illustration of the medieval-realist element in the conservative mind than Burke's defense of *corporate* ownership of property under the *ancien regime:* property held in both deed and historical tradition by the great semi-public ecclesiastical and civil foundations, including the monasteries, universities and charitable institutions. In the name of natural rights individualism, the Jacobin rulers declared corporate property non-existent in as much as, under natural law theory, only individuals could hold proper title to property. On this Burke waxes sarcastic. When Henry VIII had robbed the monasteries, he had at least gone through the motions of having a commission find or pretend to find obliquities in monastic rule. But he did not and could not, know what

> an effectual instrument of despotism was to be found in that grand magazine of offensive weapons, the rights of men.... Had fate reserved him to our times, four technical terms would have done his business, and saved him all this trouble: he needed nothing more than one short form of incantation— *Philosophy, Light, Liberality, the Rights of Men.*

There is in conservative theory of private property a strong Roman character. Property is more than external appendage to man, mere inanimate servant of human need. It is, above anything else in civilization, the very condition of man's humanness, his superiority over the entire natural world. Not, the Roman argument goes, until a human being, at some time in the remote past, took a piece of earth for himself and declared 'This is mine,' was it possible for man's sovereignty over the earth and all that lay on it to assert itself and thus become the first step in the development of civilization. In Roman Law, especially in the original tables and in the law of the Republic, the root, and essential, meaning of *familia* is property—real property; land, foremost, but all property that is in the hereditary possession of the *patria potestas,* the law of the household. Property could never be alienated from the family line save as the consequence, determined by the Senate, of grievous and imperishable crime. All through the Republic, any *individual* right to property was not so much repudiated as simply unknown and therefore unimaginable. It was under the Empire, beginning with the Caesars, that family control of property began to erode away and individual rights to family inheritance multiply.

The whole essence of the conservative view of property, and of the strongly Roman-feudal component of this view, is to be seen of course in the customs and laws of primogeniture and entail. Both were designed to protect the *family* character of property, to save it from becoming the uncertain, possibly transitory, possession of the individual alone. Almost everything about the medieval law of family and marriage, including the stringent emphasis upon chastity of the female, the terrible penalty that could be exerted against adultery by the wife, springs from a nearly absolute reverence for property, for legitimate heritability of property. So far as the inauguration of modernity is concerned in Western history, the abolition of the laws of entail and primogeniture will do as well as any single cause of the Great Transformation.

So deeply impressed was Tocqueville by the crucial role of the family-property molecule in history that he saw the *real* American Revolution as being, not the events comprising the Revolutionary War against Great Britain, but rather the profound changes made almost immediately after the Revolution by the new states' legislatures in the nature of property. Without exception, those states in which primogeniture and entail, elements of the English colonial heritage, still existed when the new republic was born, acted swiftly to abolish these ancient traditions. Tocqueville thought that the death of primogeniture and entail, to be replaced by 'equal partition of property,' could have only one result: 'the intimate connection is destroyed between family feeling and the preservation of the paternal estate; the property ceases to represent the family.' From this dissolution, this smashing of the family-property molecule, came, Tocqueville thought, much of the *egoisme* and *individualisme* that he believed he saw over the American landscape. 'Where family pride ceases to act, individual selfishenss comes into play. When the idea of family becomes vague, indeterminate, and uncertain, a man thinks of his present convenience; he provides for the establishment of his next succeeding generation and no more.' As is so often the case in Tocqueville's *Democracy in America,* it is not so much America he is really thinking about in these words as it is his fellow-French, but the essential point is the same.

Tocqueville, it can be added here, reveals himself in his *Recollections,* a memoir of his experiences in the French legislature during the revolution of 1848, as a conservative of the first order. He voted regularly with the propertied class as a legislator; he espoused completely *laissez-faire,* seeing the 'laws of commerce' as 'the laws of God;' he took Nassau Senior as his model economist, not his own friend John Stuart Mill; he was contemptuous of the 'deluded' people who thought government could mitigate misfortune that was caused by Providence; he excoriated Lamartine, head of government, for not dispersing with armed force the crowds of unemployed massed around the legislative building; and finally he was a strong admirer of Edmund Burke.

He might well have been, for Burke too was an apostle of *laissez-faire.* The final part of *Reflections on the Revolution in France* is taken up almost exclusively with the evils produced by the Jacobin philosophy of government, one that mandated scheme after scheme for direct use of government power and revenue in the economic, social and moral affairs of the people. In his *Thoughts and Details on Scarcity,* in which we have already seen a strict philosophy of localism and decentralization, the recommendation is the same when it comes to the possible role of government in time of famine or other crisis in the lives of the people.

> To provide for us in our necessities is not in the power of Government. It would be a vain presumption in statesman to think they can do it. The people maintain them, not they the people. It is in the power of Government to prevent much evil; it can do very little positive good in this, *or perhaps in any thing else.* (Italics added)

But what, Burke asks himself, 'if the rate of hire to the labourer comes far short of his necessary subsistence, and the calamity of the time is so great as to threaten actual famine?' Burke remains sternly consistent.

> In that case, my opinion is this. Whenever it happens that a man can claim nothing according to the rules of commerce, and the principles of justice, he passes out of that department, and comes within the jurisdiction of mercy. In that province the magistrate has nothing at all to do; his interference is a violation of the property which it is his office to protect. Without all doubt, charity to the poor is direct and obligatory upon all Christians, next in order after the payment of debts, full as strong, and by nature made infinitely more delightful to us...

Charity is, then, for Burke, an obligation of church, as it is of family and village or neighborhood, but never of the government.

The cry of the people in cities and towns, though unfortunately (from a fear of their multitude and combination) the most regarded, ought in *fact* to be the *least* attended to upon this subject; for citizens are in a state of utter ignorance of the means by which they are to be fed, and they contribute little or nothing ... to their own maintenance.

Try as we may, we find little if anything—besides adroit party tactical maneuvering—to offset Burke's position when we turn to Disraeli. That he wanted, and eventually got, a mass constituency for the Conservative Party says nothing in itself about a philosophy of charity or welfare. He was vastly more interested in using this electoral base for the strengthening of crown, aristocracy, and church than for anything directly improving the lives of the indigent and suffering. He got the mass base for his party in 1867, and when, after becoming Prime Minister, he introduced reform bills in 1874, they were hardly the stuff of popular welfare. They were mostly concerned with sanitation, and Disraeli's own wry, self-mocking comment upon his 'reform' bills was: *Sanitas sanitatum, omnia sanitas.* Beyond sanitation the bills concerned some shrewd redistricting of voters and contracts between employers and employees.

Disraeli's latest and best biographer Robert Blake writes: 'Like all politicians of his era, Disraeli had to trim his sails to the 'liberal' wind ... . Many Conservative leaders have had a hankering for Disraeli's precept, but have usually followed Peel's practice—and so did Disraeli.' Blake continues: 'He was perhaps unlucky or unwise in adumbrating any Tory "philosophy" at all....For it gave his enemies the opportunity of pointing out that he did very little to carry it into practice when in power...'

The origin of the still existent belief that Disraeli was at heart a Tory socialist seems to lie in his brief and only half-interested association in the 1840s with Lord Manners and George Smythe, two youthful Tories fresh from Eton and Cambridge, eager for recognition in the House of Commons, who founded what became known as 'Young England.' This was a small movement that sought to undo the influence in England of the utilitarians and the factory owners. Robert Blake, in his history of the Conservative Party, writes: 'This possibility appealed particularly to idealists, romantics, escapists, all who harked back to a largely imaginary pre-industrial golden age.' Young England did not last long. Even its founder, Manners, came to a rather drastic change of mind. His earliest recommendation for Manchester was that it adopt a form of monasticism. But he came to see, after a visit to Lancashire, that the proprietorial tie in the mills was nothing but a new and promising form of feudalism. 'There was never so complete a feudal system,' he wrote, as that of the mills; soul and body are or might be at the disposal of one man, and that to my mind is not at all a bad state of society.' It was not a bad way either to end 'Young England,' though it did have something of a resurrection at the end of the century in a tiny group of Tory politicians led by Randolph Churchill, Winston's father, among whom the conceit of a 'Fourth Party' gave a little lift to life. Blake gives them decent burial: 'Neither Young England nor the Fourth Party achieved anything significant, but their memory will always beckon to those incurable romantics too whom political life is something more than a humdrum profession.'

We do no better in any search for a Tory vein of welfarism when we turn to John Henry Newman. The only thing he ever published on public policy was *Who's To Blame?* in 1855. It addressed itself to the crisis in England brought on by Crimean disasters. There are some trenchant observations on the natural susceptibility of a people to panic in time of emergency that has in its recent past known too much 'participation' in government and not enough of its protective authority. In the main, Newman's excellent work is a strong defense of the English constitution, a defense that has a great deal in it of the philosophy of Burke, whom Newman, like Disraeli, revered. But one must strain indeed to find a suggestion of governmental policy in welfare matters that differs from Burke's. Newman had the same veneration for property and aristocracy that Burke and Disraeli had. He had little appetite for reform, citing Wellington's question in his opposition to the Reform Bill of 1832: 'How is the King's Government to be carried on?

Bismarck is often hailed as the true 'father of the modern welfare state,' but as with Disraeli, evidence is hard to come by. He instigated his bills for unemployment and sickness insurance solely to frustrate and weaken the pestiferous, Bebel-led Socialists—in which he succeeded. But so little did Bismarck, the quintessential conservative Prussian Junker, think of his bills, that there is no mention of them in his copious memoirs. Those bills bore about as much relation to Bismarck's philosophy as Churchill's escapade in 1909, when he bolted party and supported Lloyd George's near revolutionary budget, did to his life-long convictions. In 1909 Churchill actually joined in the support of the emasculation of the House of Lords, even in support of some temperance measures then before the House. But whatever his motivations then, substantial and lasting change in his very conservative ideology of government was not one of them. Somehow he managed to suffer Stalin's and the Soviet Union's embraces—or rather his embraces of them—during the second World War. But the war had barely ended, as had his wartime comradeship with Socialists Attlee and Bevin among others, when in an early campaign speech for reelection he declared: 'There can be no doubt that Socialism is inseparably interwoven with totalitarianism and the abject worship of the State.' To which he added his conviction that a Socialist government in Britain would quickly invoke a 'Gestapo-like' secret police. That was the authentic Churchill, the Burkean Churchill, the Churchill of boundless devotion to landed property, to aristocracy, to monarchy, and empire.

None of what I have written on conservatism and property—and on social welfare—is intended to imply that conservatives are thereby, necessarily, indifferent about the plight of the indigent and the miserable. Their argument may be stated easily: There are groups beginning with the family and including the neighborhood and church, which are duly constituted to render assistance, and in the form of *mutual-aid,* not high-flown charity from a bureaucracy. Such groups are mediating bodies by nature; they are closer to the individual and in their very communal strength natural allies of the individual. The primary purpose of government is to look to the conditions of strength of these groups, in as much as they are by virtue of ages of historical development the best fitted to deal with the majority of problems in individuals' lives. But to bypass these groups through welfare aid addressed directly to designated classes of individuals is, conservatism argues, at once an invitation to discrimination and inefficiency and a relentless way of eroding the significance of the groups. Disuse and atrophy apply very well indeed to social evolution. Lamennais put it well: Centralization creates apoplexy at the center and anemia at the extremities. This, and most especially in welfare matters, has been historically and *mutatis mutandis* remains the conservative position.

'The relations of groups of men to plots of land,' wrote Namier, 'form the basic content of political history.' Even when it is not land, it is more likely to be *hard* property, property in the forms of tangible, visible, essentially unconcealable *things,* beginning with the soil itself, rather than the 'soft' kinds of property contained in notes, bonds, debentures and credit. In conservative writing throughout the nineteenth century, on both sides of the Atlantic, there is a strongly feudal cast given to property and to the relation between it and the human community. Disraeli in a general preface to his novels, wrote in 1870: 'The feudal system may have worn out, but its main principle—that the tenure of property should be the fulfillment of duty—is the essence of good government.' Not from the state as hand-out, but from the very bond, the chain, of human association as rooted in property, must come charity and mutual aid. To the present moment, a more or less democratized variant of that dogma is part of the essence of conservatism everywhere in Western society.

To a very large extent, this feudal view of human interdependence was and is based upon the kind of hard property that is anchored in land. Burke knew this and it explains his eloquently expressed anger at the actions of the 'monied interests' in France as well as the laws and decrees against family, class and property from the Jacobins. He believed he saw a link between the two forces.

> In this state of real, though not always perceived warfare between the noble ancient landed interest, and the new monied interest, the greatest because most applicable strength was in the hands of the latter. The monied interest is in its nature more ready for any adventure; and its possessor more disposed to new enterprises of any kind....It is therefore the kind of wealth which will be resorted to by all who wish for change.

Tocqueville shared in full Burke's animosity toward fluid, mobile, monied property; but instead of excoriating it directly, he settled for identification of it as one of the 'major causes of that instability which must always attend the middle class in its aspirations.' A true landed class in America was improbable, Tocqueville thought, because the 'fever of speculation' is to be found even in those, whether wealthy or not, who turn to the land. People in democracies see the land not as a basis of a way of life but as a commodity to rise and fall in commercial value. Historically, land had justified itself, Tocqueville and most conservatives thought, by its inseparability, as a form of wealth, from a high degree (however reluctant in some instances) of social and economic responsibility. That is, land, as the economic base of society, required a large number of retainers to cultivate and maintain it. Jobs for the people were thus built into landed wealth.

But this was far from true of softer forms of wealth, found in shares and notes. Lecky, in his *Democracy and Liberty,* observed the unhappy conversion of landed estates to mere pleasure resorts for their owners under the new economic order that rested on business and finance. 'Country places taken for mere pleasure and unconnected with any surrounding property or any landlord duties will be more frequent.'

Struggle between the two kinds of property, landed and financial, hard and soft, has been one of the epics in American history. The squatter and homesteader in the West could fight against government and financial speculator as determinedly as the owner of vast cattle ranges. If nothing quite like the European and Asiatic passion for the land, for soil of any kind or dimension, ever grew up in America, it is nevertheless a side of American life not to be neglected. However unconscious the trust in land and other hard property may have been in the minds of those who fought their battles for it, there was a certain wisdom in the fight. It is far easier, as Burke and every other conservative has known, to instill a sense of the value of order in each citizen, and to encourage his sense of the true values of liberty when he has an overriding sense of holding a 'stake in society.' And such 'stake' is never so pressing on one's conscience as when it is in the form of land, or lacking that, very hard property. From the landed aristocrat and the peasant in the Middle Ages down to the proprietor and the home-owner of our own day, the principle of the stake-in-society has rarely been upset.

It was in full sense of this truth that the conservative Joseph Schumpeter, in *Capitalism, Socialism, and Democracy,* warned us that the work of advancing socialism, and of social democracy generally, would be made all the easier by certain erosive forces attending property which were already well advanced in capitalist society. 'The capitalist process, by substituting a mere parcel of shares of the walls of and the machines in a factory, takes the life out of the idea of property.' So attenuated would become the idea of, and faith in, property, Schumpeter concluded, that the will to defend it would die and with this the will to defend other individual freedoms. Let current forces work their way much longer in the erosion of the sense of property, concluded Schumpeter, and when transition to socialism takes place, 'the people will not even be aware of it.'

Yet another aspect of the conservative philosophy of property in modern history is found in the frequent criticisms of capitalism, together with its industrialism, commerce, and technology, by conservatives. As I have stressed above, conservatism is almost as much a response to the industrial as the democratic revolution at the end of the eighteenth century. Even before Burke wrote the *Reflections* there was a substantial body of traditionalist opinion in Western Europe that included factories and mines in its indictment of modernism, referring to them often as the 'English system.' There is little if anything of this to be found in Burke. So much like his cherished friend Adam Smith was he that he referred to the 'laws of commerce' as being quite as 'eternal' as any of the natural laws of man. Burke, so perceptive in most things, was quite unaware of the sheer irony that lay in his sentimental reference to 'the tenant-right of a cabbage-garden' in the *Reflections* and to the 'ceremonious' treatment of this right by Parliament. For that body, through dozens, even hundreds of enclosure acts was systematically destroying tenant rights to cabbage-gardens in the interests of a new class of first landed, then industrial capitalists.

But Burke aside, criticism of capitalism, of the new economic order generally, is rife in nineteenth-century conservative writing. Coleridge made plain his distrust of 'commerce' and the impersonal identification of human beings by their property status. He based his argument for the supremacy of a 'clerisy' in large part on the 'tearing, rending, and shattering' effects of commerce and industry upon the historic social bond. Southey, in his *Letters From England,* published in 1807, reads like a late nineteenth-century socialist in his indictment of the ills brought upon England by the factory system and the hideously congested towns and cities resulting from this system. In the new towns Southey saw, at first hand, obliquities and infections without precedent in the working class quarters. 'Utterly uninstructed in the commonest principles of religion and morality, they were as debauched and profligate as human beings under the influence of such circumstances must inevitably be.' Disraeli, in almost total agreement with his revered Coleridge, expressed his hatred of 'a sort of spinning-jenny, machine kind of nation.' With much reason, at the end of the century, G. B. Shaw commented on how much fiercer many conservative criticisms of capitalism were than were those of Marxian socialists. The reason is apparent. The Marxians at least accepted the technical framework of capitalism for their coming socialism. For conservatives in many instances, that was the loathsome part of it all.

In France, the conservatives, with Bonald leading the way, saw commerce, industry, and large cities as just as subversive of 'constituted' society as the natural rights doctrines of the Jacobins. In an interesting essay on the comparative effects upon the family and neighborhood of rural and urban life, Bonald rejected the latter on the ground that it increased the social distance between individuals, loosened the bonds of marriage and family, and gave a moneyed character to all life that was not present in a landed-agrarian rural society. In traditional society, Bonald stressed, the very nature of work required an unconscious strengthening of family and cooperation among people. He wrote: 'Urban life brings physical proximity but social distance among its inhabitants. In rural life the people are physically far apart but socially together.' Late in the century, a whole school of sociology would arise on essentially that insight. And throughout the century, in the works of Chateaubriand, Balzac, Flaubert, Brunetiere and Bourget—profoundly conservative—there was a running assault upon the individualism, the secularism, the social disorganization, that capitalism, quite as much as popular democracy, threatened the lives of human beings.

Not later than the 1820s, and largely through the brilliant Lamennais, in the beginning ultramontane Catholic as well as monarchist, the attention of the Roman Catholic Church was fatefully brought to the phenomenon of capitalism. There would be of course bishops and cardinals friendly to urban-industrial life, capable of seeing it as important to the welfare of many millions of people. But from the 1820s down to the present moment there is to be seen a vivid strain of liberationism, egalitarianism, and socialism or social democracy in the Catholic world that made capitalism its enemy, that looked to a 'distributivist' rather than capitalist society, and that had a powerful effect in Europe in the generating of trade union and cooperative defenses against individualistic capitalism. It is instructive that even at the turn of the century, Charles Maurras, whose conservatism reached the very heights of reaction, made capitalism and its plutocrats as guilty as radical democrats and socialists of the destruction of traditional society.

But we cannot close this section without emphasizing again that irrespective of variant conservative attitudes toward capitalism, or any other more or less concrete mode of economy, the philosophy of conservatism has been adamant on the sanctity of property. In the heart of every true conservative there is, as Russell Kirk properly writes, 'persuasion that property and freedom are inseparably connected, and that economic levelling is not economic progress. Separate property from private possession and liberty is erased.' Irving Babbitt took it farther: 'Every form of social justice ...tends toward confiscation, and confiscation, when practiced on a large scale, undermines moral standards, and, in so far, substitutes for real justice the law of cunning and the law of force.'

Even in our age, in the declining years of century and millennium, when the liberal-socialist principles of the welfare state have become the conventional wisdom of almost all citizens by now, when inroads into once-sacrosanct property have been indelibly made by Burke's 'monied interests' and 'new dealers' as well as by the legislators and bureaucrats he labelled 'political theologians' and 'theological politicians' even now the surest insight into the liberal, the socialist, and the conservative mind, the most certain means of identifying each genus, is the test of property. Rightly did the Romans, and then again medieval aristocrats and peasants alike, see property as but an extension of the human body, as precious as limb and life. To Richard Weaver, often called the morning star of the contemporary renascence of conservative thought in the United States, property is 'the last metaphysical right.' But even Weaver, passionate foe of the liberal and the socialist, found the modern corporation and novel forms of private property hard to accept as a way of life. 'We are looking,' Weaver wrote, 'for a place where a successful stand may be made for the logos against modern barbarism. It seems that small scale property offers such an entrenchment, which is of course a place of defense. Yet offensive operations too must be undertaken.'

The memory and the dream of hard property, best of all, landed property, and of property not become corporately vast and amorphous, remain firm in the conservative mind. For conservatives the thought of a corporation like AT&T prior to recent divestiture, as big as many a sovereign government on earth, with employees numbering many hundreds of thousands and with several million stockholders, can be as difficult to accept as is the whole Federal bureaucracy. It is no wonder that many conservatives of the Western United States regard the Northeast and its headquarters for hundreds of great corporations as somehow less than genuinely conservative, as verg-

ing on the liberal. The 1964 contest between Nelson Rockefeller
and Barry Goldwater in the Republican Party epitomized this.

Religion and Morality

Conservatism is unique among major political ideologies in its
emphasis upon church and the Judaeo-Christian morality. All of the
early conservatives, and no one more deeply than Burke, were hor-
rified by the Jacobin blows to the Church in France. Reference to
these, and correlatively to the vital role of religion in the good society, takes up more pages in the *Reflections* than any other single
subject with the possible exception of property. So too did the establishment of religion in the state matter greatly. For Burke the established religion was of course the Anglican faith, although his mother
had been a devout Roman Catholic and he himself gave much attention to the plight of Roman Catholics in Great Britain. Bonald, de
Maistre, and Chateaubriand chose the Roman Catholic religion for
legitimate establishment. But irrespective of denomination, all the
conservatives, Hegel, Haller, Coleridge included, made religion a
very keystone of state and society.

It is the institutional aspect of religion that is alone germane here
to political conservatism. It would be absurd to credit conservatives
in the nineteenth century with greater personal religious devotion
than liberals. No major conservative of the period wrote as passionately and committedly on Christianity as did the liberal, pro-Jacobin,
genius-scientist Joseph Priestley. He was far from alone among scientists—for example, Faraday and Maxwell—or among those who
identified with political liberalism or served ultimately liberal and
social democratic purposes, as did the Wesleyans.

Priestley's was an evangelical, millennialist Christianity, with heavy
stress upon the Calvinist virtues of inner grace and also knowledge
of and devotion to the Bible as God's literal word. This is assuredly
not the case with any of the founding fathers of political conservatism: not with Burke, Coleridge, Southey, Disraeli and Newman in
England or with Bonald, de Maistre and Chateaubriand in France.
Religion for them was preeminently public and institutional, something to which loyalty and a decent regard for form were owing, a
valuable pillar to both state and society, but not a profound and per-
meating doctrine, least of all a total experience. That kind of religion
marked the Dissenters, Burke thought – and this he repeatedly wrote

in his letters. His own faith in religious establishment led Burke to take a distinctly troubled view of religious enthusiasm such as that of the Dissenters. They, of course, were deadly enemies of Establishment, and were far from being above the uses of violence against Anglicans. It was on precisely this that one of Burke's most revealing letters was written, to his friend Dr Erskine. Dr Erskine had sent a number of copies of Scottish Dissenter sermons to reassure Burke that these preachers specifically rejected violence in advocacy of their cause of Disestablishmentarianism. Burke, clearly, was not impressed; and his words could be used unchanged at this moment in application to extreme anti-abortionists in America:

> To represent a man as immoral by his religion, perfidious by his principles, a murderer on point of conscience, an enemy from piety to the foundations of all social intercourse, and *then* to tell us that we are to offer no violence to such a person under favor, appears to me rather an additional insult and mockery than any sort of corrective of the injury we do our neighbor by the character we give him.

Burke was valiant in his efforts to give the Dissenters their full civil rights, but it is easy enough to draw the conclusion that he regarded them as just short of public nuisances, ever on the verge of carrying enthusiasm to public disorder and to arousal of hate for those who disagreed with them. Burke was remarkably free of religious prejudice. He is speaking of the Dissenters in the following:

> My ideas of toleration go far beyond theirs. I would give a full civil protection, in which I include an immunity, from all disturbance of their public religious worship and a power of teaching in schools as well as temples, to Jews, Mahometans, and even pagans; especially if they are already possessed of any of those advantages by long and prescriptive usage, which is as sacred in this exercise of rights as in any other.

In his indictment of Lord Hastings for his abuses of the Indian people and their customs Burke declared the Muslim and Hindu writs in India to be the equal in morality and humanity of Christianity. On an occasion when a group of Indians was visiting London and had been unable to win the assent of Anglican or Dissenter alike to brief use of a church for their own religious services, Burke extended the use of his house for this purpose.

Whether one wishes to call it indifference or tolerance is hardly the question. It is quite possible that Burke and Disraeli, and many other members of the Church of England were, as some said, simply tone-deaf when it came to matters of personal faith. It is possible that each had a deep and indispensable faith in God. We do not know. Burke, in another letter, wrote: 'I do not aspire to the glory of being a distinguished zealot for any national church until I can be more certain than I am that I can do it honor by my doctrine or my life.'

But faith or lack of faith in religion has nothing to do with the position on religious establishment that most English and some American conservatives held. That position was, and still is in a surprising number of cases, inseparable from the institutional, civil aspect of establishment. Establishment served two major functions: first, it conferred a certain sacredness upon vital functions of government and upon the whole political or social bond. It might be remembered here that even Rousseau, arch-enemy of Christianity and other revealed religions, prescribed in his *Social Contract* a 'civil religion,' one that would celebrate citizenship. And the Jacobins at the height of the Revolution were more than willing to accept this among the other teachings of Rousseau. Secondly, an established, meaning a prominently featured and inevitably strong church, would act as a check upon the power of the state, upon any of its acts of 'arbitrary power.' Burke wrote:

> The consecration of the state by a state religious establishment is necessary ...to operate with an wholesome awe upon free citizens; because, in order to secure their freedom, they must enjoy some determinate portion of power. To them therefore a religion connected with the state and with their duty towards it, becomes even more necessary than in such societies where people by the terms of their subjection are confined to private sentiments.

Just before that passage there is another that demonstrates even more clearly the pluralist, essentially equilibrist view Burke took of church and state:

> We are resolved to keep an established church, an established monarchy, an established aristocracy, and an established democracy, each in the degree it exists, and in no greater.

The church is established, then, in precisely the same way that government, the social order, and the people are established. Each is inevitably the restraint upon the other, no one more, no one less. There are many indications, starting with his speeches on the American colonies, of Burke's realization of the ease with which government can move into oppressiveness. In a famous paragraph Burke declared that even the aristocracy—which at its best he saw as the true basis of society and certainly of the Whig Party—is intrinsically as prone to evil as good and that only its ingrained tradition and discipline can lead to the common weal. Democracy is no less considered by Burke in light of need for restraints by church and other institutions upon it.

A substantially similar view of establishment of religion governed the views of the French, Swiss and German conservatives. The great, indeed sufficing aim of Bonald in his *Theory of Power,* was that of restoring the Catholic church to some of the autonomy and internal authority it had had prior to the Revolution and that had only partially been returned by Napoleon in the Concordat. It is Bonald the political scientist as much as Roman Catholic who divides 'legitimate' society into the three spheres of government, church and family, each destined to be sovereign within its own realm. There is almost nothing in Bonald—the same is true of De Maistre and Chateaubriand—about Catholic faith or dogma; but a great deal about the right of the Catholic Church to all due autonomy in the realm. Lamennais, in the full blush of his youthful faith in Christianity, and for some years as brilliant prelate, took a more mystical view of the individual's relation to the Church. But his classic *Essay on Indifference,* in 1817 while he was engaged in nothing else but the furtherance of Catholic interest, is overwhelmingly institutional and historical in content. There must be, he wrote, an ultramontane Church, an established and fully recognized church, or else Europe will plunge into the abyss of unbelief, periodically 'saved' by this or that passing secular enthusiasm.

In very large degree the conservative support of religion rested upon the well-founded belief that human beings, once they have got loose from major orthodoxy, are likely to suffer some measure of derangement, of loss of equilibrium. Religion, Burke wrote in a letter to his son, 'is man's fastness in an otherwise incomprehensible and thereby hostile world.' Tocqueville, whose personal faith in Rome was real but decidedly unobtrusive before his death bed confession, admirably described the value of religion to government and society—and to freedom:

> When there is no longer any principle of authority in religion anymore than in politics, men are speedily frightened at the aspect of unbounded independence. The constant agitation of all surrounding things alarms and exhausts them.... For my part, I doubt whether man can ever support at the same time complete religious independence and entire political freedom. And I am inclined to think that if faith be wanting in him, he must be subject; and if he be free, he must believe.

Tocqueville's words doubtless fit the views of the majority of conservatives as well as any possibly could. Disraeli was born a Jew but brought into the Anglican church by his father after he had become enraged by his rabbi and broke altogether with formal Judaic belief. We know that Disraeli was a regular attender of Anglican services, accepting communion, but we know also that far from ever seeking to conceal his Jewish origin, he took pride in it and exclaimed throughout his life of the greatness of the 'Judaic race' and the profundity and the truth in Judaic gospel. But as to belief, to real commitment, he was, as his biographer Robert Blake writes, 'curiously hazy.' 'His Christianity did not fit into any ordinary category... It is probably hopeless to extract a coherent body of doctrine from his observations on religion. He believed in different things at different times and failed to see their inconsistency.'

A careful study would undoubtedly reveal that a considerable number of staunch conservatives, disciples to a man of Edmund Burke, had a regard for religion ranging from the indifferent to the outrightly hostile. Such views, including agnosticism and atheism, seem to have mattered surprisingly little to Victorians. Robert Ingersoll, staunch conservative Republican and pillar of bar and bourse, was a militant atheist. H. L. Mencken and Albert Jay Nock, both enemies of socialism, social democracy and political liberalism, both almost devout in belief in the minimal state and in the fewest possible social functions of the state—manifested in the repudiation by both of Roosevelt and the New Deal—were opponents of Christianity. So was Irving Babbitt and Paul Elmer More, though the latter somewhat unenthusiastically in later years. But all of them would doubtless have agreed with Tocqueville that some bulwark of faith, even if in a body of morality that is falsely credited with divine inspiration, is necessary to human beings and a means of saving them from the worst of the consequences of being among the alienated. Chesterton would surely have won assent from all conservatives in his words: 'The danger of loss of faith in God is not that one will then believe in nothing, but rather that one will believe in anything.' There is no need to remind readers of the degree to which Marxism, Freudianism, and other major systems of clamantly secular belief have ended up as religions themselves for a great many Westerners.

It is religion as *civil* religion that seems to be the closest to a common essence of conservative belief, religion in which a transcendental core manifests itself in civil as well as religious garments, one in which the most sacred feast days—such as Thanksgiving, Christmas, Easter, and New Year's Day—all serve religious and civil ends alike. What Tocqueville found in America in 1830—the American Religion—was in almost equal parts Christian (Puritan specifically) and nationalist. Christ the Redeemer and America the Redeemer Nation existed side by side. In that sense, then, America continued to have an 'established' church long after the American states had cut free of Christian denominations.

Conservatives have for the most part believed in the Divine much as all educated people believe in gravity or the spherical shape of the earth—firmly but not ecstatically. The hatred of 'enthusiasm' in the Dissenters and in the Wesleyans in the nineteenth century in England by most Anglicans, was shared in full by just about all conservatives. Religion is acceptable: it is indeed a good thing provided it is not made the base of the intrusion of personal beliefs into the public body of the nation. Doubtless no conservative, in the Burkean sense, has ever lived who could look out on today's Moral Majority with equanimity, what with its so often brazen and calculated confusion of the secular—as manifested by intrusive laws and constitutional amendments—and the transcendentally religious. Even T. S. Eliot, who accepted Anglican establishment along with royalism and traditionalism, warned, in his *Idea of a Christian Society,* of the dangers inherent in a religious establishment that is not founded upon powerful and widespread currents of religious history. You cannot have, Eliot wrote, 'a national Christian society ... if it is constituted as a mere congeries of private and independent sects.' Moreover, 'A permanent danger of an established church is Erastianism ... the danger that a National Church might become also a nationalistic church.'

In our day Michael Oakeshott has admirably stated the Burkean, and indeed the whole conservative, view of the proper relation between government and individual morality:

> Thus, governing is recognized as a specific and limited activity.... It is not concerned with concrete persons, but with activities; and with activities only in respect of their propensity to collide with one another. It is not concerned with moral right and wrong, it is not designed to make men good or even better; it is not indispensable on account of the "natural depravity of mankind" but merely because of their current disposition to be extravagant.

Doubtless that is what Burke had in mind when he said: 'Politics and the pulpit are terms that have no agreement. No sound ought to be heard in the Church but the healing voice of Christian charity.'

3

Some Consequences of Conservatism

No one acquainted with the history of modern European thought can fail to mark the difference between the eighteenth and nine-teenth centuries in respect to the thinking in the two centuries about man and society. There are persistences of the eighteenth-century mind, of course. *Individual, state* and *civilization* are all luminous in the nineteenth century. Individualism remains a clamant voice in almost all political discussions, with utilitarianism replacing for the most part natural law theory. The prominence of what the French had called *la patrie*—the nurturing state—is as evident as ever in the swirling currents of humanitarianism, socialism and social democ-racy. Although the starkness of the concept of civilization is relieved a good deal by the fascination with *society* as master-concept, there is no want of writing about civilization in the nineteenth century, usually, now, as contrast to the anthropologists' primitive culture.

But the differences between the two centuries vastly outweigh the likenesses. In the first place, most of the apparatus of natural law is gone completely, replaced from the beginning of the nineteenth cen-tury by a set of closely related concepts the foundation of which was not the natural but instead the *social*; that is, the complex of *actual* ties and bonds among human beings which were the deposit of his-torical development, which were manifest in institutions and cus-toms, and which had been so largely scorned by natural law think-ers under the impress of their fascination with the supposed natural atoms of human nature and behavior—atoms, as they believed, which were comparable to those which physical philosophers had discov-ered by simply ignoring the world of sense and going straight to the hard, unchanging elements of reality.

As we have seen, at the heart of Burke's and other early conservatives' indictment of the Revolutionists and the *philosophes,* lay a total disbelief in the existence of a presocial world of this sort. It was this world of alleged natural forces and patterns to which the conservatives directed their accusations of metaphysicality, of preoccupation with the imaginary at the expense of the historically real.

Gunnar Myrdal, no conservative, has written in our time to this point. 'The conservative wing profited from its idealism. In its practical work it abstained from speculating about a "natural order" other than the one that existed; it studied society as it was, and actually came to lay the foundation of the modern social sciences.' Myrdal is generally correct, I believe, but we must not forget the precipitating circumstances of the conservative *Aufklärung.* They did not include any passion for simple scientific objectivity. They were inseparable from the attack the conservatives mounted on natural law philosophy in the name of the historically evolved fabric of conventions, customs, prejudices, and institutions to which their patriotic emotions were exclusively directed. The point is, the conservatives were instrumental in *identifying* the world of institutions and their growths —identifying this world for the uses of nineteenth-century scholarship and science—simply by virtue of their sustained *eulogy* of it at the expense of the hated, 'metaphysical' world of natural law and natural rights.

Suddenly there took place a change in the style of political and social thought at least as great as the changes in style which literary and art historians discover and which lead to the various epochs and ages into which works of art and literature are placed. The difference between the 'classical' and the 'romantic' in the arts is no greater, it seems to me, than the difference between the style of eighteenth- and nineteenth-century political thought.

The new style is evidenced in its language. It is impossible to miss the newly found popularity of the many synonyms, derivations and empirical manifestations of the social—and in a short time the cultural, which in its anthropological reference was as new and encompassing in the nineteenth century as the social. As words, *social, tradition, custom, institution, folk, community, organism, tissue,* and *collective* achieved almost overnight a prestige and function they had not known since the heyday of realist vs. nominalist thought in the Middle Ages. We see the rise of *social* anthropology, *social* psychology, *social* geography and economics—not to forget *sociology* which Auguste Comte coined as the name for what he envisaged as the master science of sciences, the science of society, and which he broke down into the two great divisions of *social statics* and *social dynamics*. Nor can we overlook the diffusion in nineteenth-century thought of *family, kindred, parish, village, social class* and *caste, status, town, church, sect,* etc., all obviously the historically formed molecules of the great reality, society. These, and not abstract, atomistic individuals of natural law fancy are the true subjects of a true science of man.

Individualism is by no means routed in the nineteenth century; the strength of utilitarianism and of instinct-psychology is proof enough of that. All the same, the idea of society, and paralleling it, of culture come close to holding sovereign place in the greater part of humanistic thinking in the century. The natural law school had sought to derive society, with its several institutions, from the individual; from the several passions or drives which, it was thought, were the motive forces of these institutions. Now, though, we find either society or culture held up as the crucial force shaping the conduct, even the very nature, of the individual. Natural law philosophers had enjoyed reducing the institutional, the social, to some aboriginal or hypothetical contract. But in several schools of legal and moral thought in the nineteenth century, the emphasis was on the social or cultural foundations of contract; any kind of contract.

The idea of progress—or development, or evolution, or growth as terminology might have it; the terms were interchangeable—reflected these changes of interest. In the preceding century, the epochs of the past by which the advancement of mankind was measured were commonly intellectual or cultural. Now they are social—with kinship, social class, community, and other social structures made central in the progress of man. The very heart of the idea of progress or development underwent change. Instead of distinct and separated epochs of ages of progress, with heroes and geniuses made responsible for the advance of civilization from one to the next, we now see—in Saint-Simon, Comte, Marx, Bagehot, Spencer and others—the effort made to derive change of advancement from internal, intrinsic forces rather than external ones. Comte thought his greatest achievement was that of reducing the forces of progress in society to the forces of equilibrium and disequilibrium: *a single law of order and progress.* This was in the nineteenth as well as in our own century the holy grail. Inevitably, therefore, progress and evolution and change generally came to resemble increasingly the kind of *growth* which is organic and which the conservatives had featured in their revolt against revolutionary or cataclysmic change.

Comte specifically credited the traditionalists, notably de Maistre and Bonald, with the founding of what he called 'social statics.' He sought to be evenhanded by giving credit to the *philosophes* for the idea of progressive advancement in time; but Comte could not hide his fundamental dislike of the authors of what he called 'the false dogmas of 1789.' And when he came to set forth his ideal commonwealth in the 1850s, traditionalist religious ideas were dominant.

The supremacy of conservative, contrasted with liberal-radical, ideas is nowhere more apparent in the century than in sociology. Frederick Le Play, a far greater figure than Comte in the actual scientific work of sociology, the identification, classification, and inductive-deductive use of field data, was just as committed to the conservatives as Comte was. Le Play was royalist, Roman Catholic, and committed deeply to the family—specifically a 'stem type' of family that was indistinguishable from the medieval group. Sainte-Beuve correctly called Le Play *'un Bonald rajeuni,'* a reborn Bonald, *'progressif* and *'scientifique.'* Bonald's essay on the rural vs. urban family noted briefly above, comes very close to being a spare ideal type for the research which Le Play pursued in detail and at length later in the century. In truth, from Bonald to Durkheim, Hegel to Toennies, there is a conservative strain to be seen in the sociology of the continent that contrasts substantially with England and the United States. More of the spirit of Burke is to be found in the thinking of Durkheim and Weber on the nature of society than of, say, Voltaire and Diderot—or Bentham.

In the fields of law and government Burkean ideas of organic structure and growth made their way in the nineteenth century. Savigny was perhaps the crucial figure in this; he had the highest respect for Burke, as did Maine. For both men and their followers in the historical-developmental school the adversary was Benthamite utilitarianism, especially the abstract and deductive analysis employed by John Austin, follower of Bentham, in his study of political sovereignty. Austin had about the same contempt for the institutional past that his master had had, and there was nothing important, he thought, about the state and its essential properties, indeed about law—after all, merely a command of the state—that could not be set forth in almost total disregard of history.

But for Maine repudiation of the historical past is fatal to any understanding of the state, property, family, or any other institution. It could be Burke *redivivus* instead of Maine writing: 'The Law of Nature has never maintained its footing for an instant before the historical method.' Nor was it merely European history that Maine used for his comparative studies. Ancient Greece, Rome, Ireland and contemporary India, all figure prominently. Maine and the other historical-, institutional-minded scholars of his day pursued history and anthropology over the once-luminous 'state of nature' for investigations of origins.

Comparison of present with past, and especially the medieval past, was rife in the century. Thus the notable typologies of status vs. contract (Maine), of organismic vs. individualistic (Gierke), *Gemeinschaft vs. Gesellschaft* (Toennies), mechanical vs. organic (Durkheim), traditional vs. rational (Weber), town vs. metropolis (Simmel), and of primary vs. secondary association (Cooley). In all of these typologies the first aim is doubtless comparative: simply to contrast two very fundamental types of society in the world, in the past and the present. The organic-contractual typology could be, and was, used as effectively in studies of India and the Middle East as in Europe. The premise of historical movement may or may not be present in such studies.

But most of the greater sociologists on the continent were quite willing to fit the typology into a philosophy of history; Toennies, Weber, Durkheim and Simmel made their respective stereotypes into models of historical movement. These were not particularly progress-oriented. Thus Weber wrote in very melancholy tones of the passage of the West from the charismatic-traditional to the rationalist-bureaucratic. So did Durkheim of solidarity, finding it necessary to resurrect the medieval guild and other forms of intermediate association for reclamation of man in modernity. Toennies increasingly made his *Gemeinschaft,* born of the Middle Ages, the touchstone of excellence in his contemplation of Germany and Europe. Simmel thought metropolis and the stranger were the sorry outcomes of European history.

All of these sociologists and many others in Europe were fascinated by still another attribute of modernity, the intellectual-political elites which had sprung up in the ruins and aftermath of the Middle Ages. Burke's hostility toward 'literary cabals' follows, as we have seen, from his conviction that these groups of intellectuals had played a dominant role in the onset and the course of the French Revolution. Their rhetoric of natural rights, their loathing of everything conducive to preservation of the old, and their ingrained suspicion of everything connected with the aristocracy and its manners typified, for Burke, the growing adversarial attitude of intellectuals everywhere in Western Europe. 'Political men of letters,' 'political theologians' and 'theological politicians' are among the terms by which Burke identifies *philosophes* and Jacobins in France and liberals like Paine and Price in England.

Burke even begins the work of a kind of sociology of the intellectual. The intellectual class is, he suggests, a product of both political and economic changes in post-medieval Europe. The gradual but inexorable breaking down of social distinctions and the rise of a new economic class, one with a more fluid form of wealth than that which had dominated traditionally in Europe, played a major part in creating a niche which rootless intellectuals could fill. They had lost their identification with aristocracy. 'What they lost in the old court protection, they endeavoured to make up by joining in a sort of incorporation of their own,' in the two academies and the Encyclopedia. Their common pursuit was the destruction of Christianity and the aristocracy. Many members of this new class stood high in the ranks of literature and science. The world had done them justice; and in favor of general talents forgave the evil tendency of their peculiar principles...

'The resources of intrigue are called in to supply the defects of argument and wit. To those who have observed the spirit of their conduct, it has long been clear that nothing was wanted but the power of carrying the intolerance of the tongue and the pen into a persecution which would strike at property, liberty, and life.'

Thus Burke's own, initiatory portrait of the intellectual in politics. He reveals this new class as essentially rootless, without 'stake in society,' highly mobile in their way of life, fluid and facile in thought, ever-ready to sell their talent to politician or businessman, close companion of the 'new monied interest' that Burke also detested, also a recent product of European history, ingrainedly rebellious toward government and establishment, criticism and hostility a very habit of mind, in a word—the word Lionel Trilling would use so influentially in 1950—'adversarial'to the very core. Burke's tendentious treatment of the class of political intellectuals he saw prior to and during the Revolution in France proved to be the first step in one of the most interesting intellectual developments of the nineteenth century, that of identifying and analyzing the role of the intellectual in modern society. If Burke's initiation of this pursuit is undisguisedly negative in tone, so, it seems, is the tone of those who followed him in the pursuit. Tocqueville, in his *Old Regime and the French Revolution,* and in the large number of notes he left at his death on 'the European Revolution,' emphasized and diversified the rather hostile view he had taken of intellectuals in his *Recollections,* his participant-observational treatment of the Revolution of 1848 and its principals. Tocqueville, if anything, outdid Burke in his cold hostility of the French intellectual class before, during and after the great Revolution.

The intellectual class even came to replace the nobility, Tocqueville suggests in the *Old Regime.* 'By the eighteenth century the French nobility had wholly lost [its] ascendancy, its prestige had dwindled with its power, and since the place it occupied was vacant, writers could usurp it with the greatest ease and keep it without fear of being dislodged.' The tone and the language are different in Tocqueville; more restrained, more analytical in style than polemical; but the underlying censure of the intellectual class is as clearly present as in Burke.

Sociological and psychological treatments of the intellectual abound in the generations after Burke and Tocqueville, mostly written by conservatives until relatively recent times. Burckhardt's immensely successful *Civilization of the Renaissance in Italy,* so often misunderstood as a eulogy to that period and its humanists, deals with the humanists in much the same merciless fashion Burke and Tocqueville had the *philosophes.* He pictures them as shallow, opinionated, rootless, alienated, hostile to all aspects of the establishment, especially the Church, and always willing to hire out for a term of service to the highest bidder, businessman or prince. Burckhardt's resistance to all entreaties by publishers to write yet another book on the Italian Renaissance is easily explainable: he detested the period and its *dramatis personae* just as much as Burke and Tocqueville detested the Revolution and its *politiques,* its Marats and Robespierres. Taine, Nietzsche, Weber and Schumpeter are only a few of the minds which, down to the present moment, have dealt seriously, whether passionately or dispassionately, with the sociology of the intellectual. As intellectuals in Europe did in fact play a steadily rising role of influence upon revolutionary events—in 1848, in 1870 with the Paris Commune, in 1905 in Russia, in the Bolshevik Revolution, and in no small degree in the rise of Fascism in Italy and of Nazism in Germany, down to the revolutionary disturbances of the 1960s—so did the sociology of the intellectual—stereotyped from Burke on as rebellious by nature—bulk ever larger in Western thought.

In his chapter 'Can Capitalism Survive?' in *Capitalism, Socialism and Democracy,* Schumpeter considers systematically the effect upon economic life of those whom Burke had castigated as 'sophisters, calculators, and economists.' Marx, Schumpeter tells us, was right in his forecast of decline for the capitalist system but wrong in his assignment of reason. The true conflict of classes is not between capitalist and worker-proletarian but between entrepreneur and intellectual. It is not the worker but the intellectual that becomes progressively alienated from the very economic system that established his importance in the first place. It is the intellectual's estrangement from the entrepreneur and from the kind of hard property necessary to maintain motivation toward the capitalist ethic that is the crucial fact in modern history. Thus the kind of forces which Burke had seen conspiring for the destruction of the landed society he adored is seen by Schumpeter as equally destructive of capitalism and of the instinct for private property. And the intellectual's 'hostility increases instead of diminishes with every achievement of the capitalist evolution.'

Liberalism and socialism are both visibly affected by conservative undercurrents in the nineteenth century. The rise of liberal pluralism and of stress upon decentralization in many quarters and of socialist interest in gilds, *syndicats,* and cooperatives is the consequence in substantial degree of the impact of Lamennais and Tocqueville on European thought in the 1830s. Mill had been significantly touched by Tocqueville's demonstration of the non-individualist, nonpolitical foundations of liberty, and of the almost inevitable destiny of democracy to a kind of benign totalitarianism unless intermediate associations, local government, religion, family and social class remained strong in the lives of individuals. So did

Lamennais and his followers, down through the Revolution of 1848, pursue essentially this line of thought.

A turn in the socialist tradition, or rather a part of the tradition, is to be seen in the writings of Proudhon and his lineal descendants. It was not a turn that affected Marx noticeably; he remained largely centralist and collectivist to the end, as has for the most part Marxism. Proudhon, however, had read and admired Bonald, and his own blueprint of socialist society is rich in family—patriarchal family—local community, confederation, and mutual aid groups, with every precaution to be taken against political centralization and bureaucracy. The anarchist wing of socialism would generally follow this essentially pluralist, decentralist, and associative pattern, culminating in Kropotkin's works in the early twentieth century. Less important perhaps but worthy of attention all the same are two other types of socialism in the nineteenth century which have clear conservative foundations: guild socialism, primarily English, and Catholic socialism in France and Germany—indeed, pretty much the whole social reform movement in Catholicism, which had a family-community emphasis not often found in Protestant social work or reform. Both are clear revolts against capitalism but also, unlike the main line of socialist thought, against the idea of unitary, collectivist socialism set in the modern nation. Both find models for the future in the Middle Ages.

Political pluralism is a liberal adaption of the early French and German conservative criticism of the unitary state and its monopoly of sovereignty. In England, Maitland, Figgis, and Vinogradov, all ardent students of medieval law and polity, and in France, Paul-Boncour, Durkheim, and Duguit, similarly oriented toward the plural and decentralist aspects of medieval law, are perhaps the best known among legal and political pluralists at the turn of the century. Laski in his early years as a scholar was strongly influenced by these minds, and his first two major books have detailed studies of de Maistre, Bismarck, Bonald, Lamennais, and both Brunetiere and Bourget in the light of their ideas on sovereignty and its legitimate relation to the profusion of group and associative life in the social order. In Germany, Otto von Gierke was by all odds the most prolific scholar in the medieval law of association and its fate in modern history. It was essentially to pluralist English circles that first Maitland and then Barker introduced via translation major segments of Gierke's pluralist scholarship.

There are other marks of the conservative-medievalist influence in the century. Rashdall's study of the medieval universities, Lea's investigation of the medieval inquisition, Fustel de Coulanges on the medieval origins of French legal and political institutions, the whole range of books in all Western countries on the village community, manor, fief, town, monastery and estate all attest to the ramification of the currents set in motion by the early conservatives. Duhem demonstrated in his history of modern science the fertility of the Middle Ages in respect to science and technology and the actual impoverishment of both in the still widely acclaimed Renaissance. Studies of medieval art, architecture and craftsmanship were legion. The appeal of the Gothic was for a time as great in the arts as it was in the novel and poem. Carlyle, Ruskin, Pugin and Morris all found in the Middle Ages the same kind of touchstone of excellence, the same models of the heroic in art and thought that Scott found of valour and chivalry and Henry Adams spiritual community. The Middle Ages became, by compulsion, the chief repository of the 'organic,' a virtue in society first commemorated by Burke in his repudiation of natural law contract and by the middle of the nineteenth century a very synonym for the good in almost anything.

In many ways the greatest contribution of conservatism was that of making the medieval-traditional the standard of excellence for assessment of art, literature, and life itself. Ever since the Renaissance ancient Greece and Rome had provided this standard, and in the eighteenth century in the West worship of the classical world was a fertile source of rationalist assault upon the Christian society around them. But although dedication to classical ideals and models continued in the nineteenth century, it was matched increasingly by another kind of dedication: that to the 'organic,' 'communal' and 'corporate' verities which could be found, it was said, in the traditions and customs left in European culture by the regular, ordered processes of continuity in history.

Romanticism in the nineteenth century seems to consist in large degree of social, cultural and mental elements which in their aggregate comprise a grand antithesis to the rationalism of the Enlightenment. Romantic literature, art and music tended to lift up medieval-conservative forces for adulation; not by terming these forces 'medieval-conservative' but by giving them strong associations with the organic, the subliminal, the unconscious, and withal a kind of wisdom superior to any yielded by sheer rational intellectualism. The union of romanticism and conservatism in the century rests upon a grand alliance between Burke's 'prejudices,' Madame de Stael's 'passions' and the German *Zeitgeist*. From these elements, which are the true sources of 'genuine,' in contrast to artificial and 'imposed,' art come a literature, painting, sculpture, music, and, yes, politics and economy far superior to anything that can be given by the abstract norms of rationalism. I am not suggesting here that all romantics in literature and philosophy were political conservatives—at least in Burkean terms—or that all conservatives, especially in England, were Romantics in artistic appreciation. But there is affinity all the same, especially on the continent, in France and Germany foremost, between Romantic stress on the prerational and the subconscious and conservative stress on the political wisdom that lies in man's habits of mind and heart.

Equally indebted to conservative fascination with the old and the traditional is the whole way of contemplating literature and art that came over so much of the nineteenth century throughout Europe. Suddenly writers and artists came to be seen as repositories of national traditions, histories and mystiques. The artist's cultural ancestors were seen as even more important in his life and work than surrounding conditions. T. S. Eliot, in the next century, would give succinct and accurate point to this new criticism in his 'Tradition and the Individual Talent.' Not only the best, writes Eliot, 'but the most individual parts of a [mature poet's] work may be those in which the dead poets, his ancestors, assert their immortality most vigorously.' There is, Eliot goes on, a 'continuous surrender' of the artist to 'the whole of the literature of his own country.... The progress of the artist is a continual self-sacrifice, a continual extinction of personality.'

Eliot's words express admirably the kind of approach to art that Madame de Stael signaled with the very title of her most famous work, published in 1800, *Literature Considered in Its Relation to Social Institutions,* a work eminently sensible of the persisting power of the past on individual writers. In this work, and perhaps even more strikingly in her study of German culture, she sees the letters and arts of a people as being just as much the outcome of history, tradition and the nation as the language people speak. So did Hegel in his philosophical studies of art and national consciousness; so in different but no less powerful fashion did Coleridge and Arnold; and so, perhaps in the greatest of nineteenth-century studies of literature and tradition, did Ferdinand Brunetiere later in the century.

Brunetiere was deeply traditionalist in his approach to culture and also, after his late conversion to Roman Catholicism, deeply moral. What is primarily important in a given work, he repeatedly argued, is the national tradition and the national morality from which the work had issued forth, 'just as a baby issues forth from the body of its mother race.' Bonald had written earlier that it is society that shapes the individual, not the individual society, and Brunetiere translates that into the individual and the *genre,* a word he made serve as *structure* within which any given work of art manifests itself and which so powerfully shapes, by its insistent ambience, the individual work. Brunetiere detested the utilitarians, the naturalists, and the individualists who had, he declared, devastated the organic ties which bind artists like all other individuals to their culture and history.

It was Brunetiere's passion for the historical development of genres in the world of creation that turned his attention to the biologists' doctrine of evolution; he even adopted Darwin's banner—despite his church's lack of enthusiasm for Darwin and Huxley—insisting that what Darwin had said about variations in nature, that we do not know or cannot know their origins, is equally true of 'variations' in culture, the kind represented by the eruptions of Aristotle, Moliere and Goethe. Brunetiere, more than any other single mind, is responsible too for a great deal of the modern interest in the *comparison* of genres, the distinctive genres of nations and civilizations in world history. What Brunetiere loathed was at once 'art for art's sake' and the then fashionable theory of the lone, solitary, alienated 'genius.' Both of these, products of utilitarianism and decadence in equal measure, disfigure, even destroy, the true worth and importance of art. Himself profoundly conservative in all respects, Brunetiere was nevertheless able, as was Frederick Le Play, to assail modernity and its individualism and naturalism through ingenious scientific observation rather than through change ringing on piety. All in all, what we see throughout the nineteenth century, and on into our own century, is the subordination of art as well as politics to the great forces of the past still living and dominating in our present.

The final, and doubtless greatest evidence of conservative impact on nineteenth-and twentieth-century thought is found in the fate of the idea of progress. Not that conservative skepticism of progress killed the idea; not by any means; but there is nevertheless a continuous line of reaction to the progressivist mentality from Burke's evocations of the Middle Ages in his assault on modernity all the way down to Dean William Inge's dour meditations in the twentieth century on the 'superstition' of progress. It is to conservatives, for the most part, in the nineteenth century that we must turn for relief from the poundings on our consciousness by such progress-intoxicated minds as Macaulay, Spencer and Darwin—even and especially Darwin—during the period. Progress, Spencer trumpeted, 'is not an accident but a necessity.' Darwin wrote: 'In all cases the new and improved forms of life tend to supplant the old and unimproved forms... [and] ... all corporeal and mental endowments will progress toward perfection.' The Whig interpretation of history served the middle class quite as well as Marx's 'iron necessity' of progress toward socialism served radical intellectuals in Germany and France.

'Thus,' writes a modern conservative, W. A. Inge, 'the superstition of progress was firmly established. To become a popular religion, it is only necessary for a superstition to enslave a philosophy. The superstition of progress had the singular good fortune to enslave at least three philosophies—those of Hegel, of Comte, and of Darwin.' To which we may properly add the names of those already cited here and for that matter the vast majority of liberals and radicals of the past two centuries. Progress has been in a great many quarters the precise equivalent in spiritual terms of Providence.

But not for conservatives. Burke, as we have seen, thought a larger national virtue lay in the European past than in the present that was rapidly being formed by the forces of democratic and economic revolution. Even before the French Revolution dominated Burke's mind, even when he was celebrating either the English Revolution of 1688 or the growing freedom of the American colonists, Burke's eye was fixed on traditions, conventions and beliefs bearing the clear imprint of the past. In one of his most quoted passages in the *Reflections* Burke declares the nation a 'partnership,' one in science, art and morality, but also one 'between those who are living, those who are dead, and those who are to be born.' It is hard to imagine any self-respecting *philosophe* of the French Enlightenment giving the dead a place equal to that of the living in his private political engineering. But much of the essence of modern conservatism is precisely defer-

ence to the dead—as the dead may be found cumulatively in tradition and custom.

Karl Mannheim, a sociologist and not necessarily a conservative,
has put the matter illuminatingly:

> For progressive thought everything derives its meaning in the last analysis from some-
> thing either above or beyond itself, from a future utopia or from its relation to a
> transcendent norm. The conservative, however, sees all the significance of a thing in
> what *lies behind* it, either its temporal past or its evolutionary germ. Where the progres-
> sive uses the future to interpret things, the conservative uses the past.

In conservatism there is an inversion of progress, of the Liberal-
radical perspective of progress. Thus the very qualities which mod-
ernists seize upon in their claim of a progressive unfolding of history—such things as technology, democracy, individualism, romanticism and equality—conservatives are much more likely to regard
with at least mixed reactions. In some degree, but only that, the conservative will say, these are benign qualities, but as often they are,
on the record, pernicious forces in life: uprooters of civility and
morals, harbingers of the masses, of despotism rooted in the people,
and of a widespread alienation of individuals from their natural
roots of identity and belonging. This was the view of Bonald as
early as 1796 in his study of authority. Following four centuries
of erosion of and revolt against the medieval tradition, there came
the Revolution, 'a terrible and salutary crisis, by means of which
nature roots out from the social body those vicious principles
which the weakness of authority had allowed to creep in.' The early
conservatives offer, in their distrust of everything that had happened
since the Middle Ages, a tragic view of history, set in sprung rhythm.
Not slow, gradual ascent, or for that matter, descent, but, rather, a
historical plane repeatedly beset by crisis. History is plural, spas-
modic, and an almost endless succession of 'organic' and 'critical'
periods, to use the words of Saint-Simon which were directly
inspired by Bonald and de Maistre. In fact, conservatives had
tended to give a good deal more emphasis to critical periods of
disorder and decadence than to their opposites. W. H. Mallock
wrote for almost all conservatives when he said in *Is Life Worth
Living?* 'Unless we know something positive to the contrary, the
outcome of all this "progress" may be nothing but a more undis-
turbed ennui or a more soulless sensuality.' In Germany,
Schopenhauer foresaw an ever more encompassing boredom, one

punctuated by escape in narcotic or violence, as the bequest of modern progress.

'Commerce,' wrote Coleridge, 'has enriched thousands, it has been the cause of the spread of knowledge and science, but has it added one particle of happiness or of moral improvement? Has it given truer insight into our duties or tended to revive and sustain us in the better feelings of our nature? No!'

Burckhardt put the matter even more strongly, as did Tocqueville toward the end of his life. Burckhardt wrote:

I have no hope at all for the future. It is possible that a few half endurable decades may still be granted to us, a sort of Roman imperial time. I am of the opinion that democrats and proletarians must submit to an increasingly harsh despotism.

In 1848, at the close of the revolution of that year in France, Tocqueville asked.

Shall we ever, as we are assured by other prophets ... attain a more complete and more far-reaching social transformation than our fathers foresaw and desired, and that we ourselves are able to foresee, or are we not destined simply to end in a condition of intermittent anarchy, the well-known chronic and incurable complaint of old peoples?

In many ways the harshest criticism of the idea of progress by conservatives was their denial of its entire perspective of history, a perspective based upon the supposition of some great entity known as mankind that is like a single individual human being living throughout time and slowly, gradually, and continuously improving itself intellectually and morally over a vast number of centuries. But this image makes better metaphor and prophecy than it does analysis and understanding: that is the essence of a large amount of conservative response to the philosophy of progressivism in the nineteenth, and indeed in the twentieth century. The upshot of progressivism in the liberal and socialist mind was the glorification of Western society as the be-all and end-all of human history. Just as biological evolution has culminated in the production of *homo sapiens*—so goes the conventional progressivist argument—social evolution has culminated in the particular composite of material and non-material elements that we call Western civilization. All the peoples who have ever lived, together with all the non-Western peoples on earth today, can be fused into one long human progression with the West securely in the forefront. That is the kind of historical idiocy that sprang up in the nineteenth century from the progress-mentality.

A great many conservatives were doubtless caught up as were liberals and radicals by this chimerical arrangement of human history. But it can be said, I think, that it was conservatives overwhelmingly who led the way in the assault upon the idea of progress—as a methodological construct as well as a eudemonic fancy. Spengler's *The Decline of the West,* written in large part before the outbreak of the First World War and thus not to be pigeon-holed as one more expression of German *Angst* after defeat, worked out a vast alternative to conventional, progressive world history; an alternative that consists of cycles. He saw the entire past of the human race, and also the present, as encapsulated in the independent cycles of about eight great civilizations, each in accord with Spengler's 'morphology of history,' and could be seen as going through birth, development, decay and eventual death. Spengler saw Western civilization as already in the senescent period of its cycle.

Both the Adams brothers saw human history in essentially concrete and cyclical terms, with degeneration, dissolution, 'entropy' or Brownian motion eventually taking over every national history including America's. Both Henry and Brooks scorned the epics of progress and the progressive schemes of social evolution which lay around them. Irving Babbitt went even farther. He rejected any conceivable kind of philosophy of history, cyclical or other. 'In spite of certain superficial resemblances in our respective views, Spengler and I are at opposite poles of human thought. My own attitude is one of extreme unfriendliness to every possible philosophy of history.' Babbitt specifically included the Christian philosophy of history but also the 'newer type which tends to make of man a puppet of nature.'

Conservative criticism of the philosophy of progress, a very center-piece of modernity, is reflective of its general role of culture-critic in the contemporary world. Its criticisms of industrialism precede those of the socialists, and they were more fundamental in that they included industrialism's technological infrastructure. And to these criticisms conservatives added their indictments of the leveling of arts and skills under the press of democracy and mass society. As I have noted above, for most conservatives socialism appeared as an almost necessary emergent of democracy and totalitarianism an almost equally necessary product of social democracy.

For many centuries philosophers and artists had gone back to the ancient classical world for models of greatness. It was the conservatives in the early nineteenth century who, without abandoning Greece and Rome, turned nevertheless to the Middle Ages and its Gothic themes for models. The most pungent contrast for conservative critics was that between the Dynamo and the Virgin, as Henry Adams phrased it, each the image of a whole culture. Conservatives have been prophets of the medieval past, as Faguet called them, but also guerrillas of the past in almost constant attacks on modernity—economic, political, and, far from least, cultural. Liberals and socialists could look to their imaginings of the future for inspiration. Conservatives, knowing well the appeal of tradition, the depth in the human mind of nostalgia, and the universal human dread of the ordeal of change, the challenge of the new, have rested their indictment of the present frankly and unabashedly on models supplied directly by the past. Tocqueville's criticisms of modernity in his *Democracy in America* have proved far more penetrating than those of Marx. In Tocqueville the specter of the feudal and aristocratic past is constantly at hand to supply relief. Nowhere in Tocqueville is this more striking than with respect to the arts and sciences, manners or 'habits of the heart,' and of culture generally.

The conservative roots—those supplied by Coleridge, Newman, Arnold and Ruskin, and in France by Brunetiere and Bourget—of cultural criticism in our age are only too evident. Not from the liberals or radicals in the last century has the appeal of the traditional, the organic, and of the distinction between culture and civilization (made so basic by Coleridge) come down to almost all critics, conservative or radical, in our age. Criticisms of the culture of modernity, whether from Eliot or Leavis, from Bertrand Russell or Spengler, all have distinct evocations in them of what Eliot called 'the usable past.' Daniel Bell has described himself as a socialist in economics, a liberal in politics, and a conservative in culture. He is far from alone. Nowhere have the guerrillas of the past been more active and successful than in the sphere of culture.

4

The Prospects of Conservatism

Conservatives might have been forgiven, however, at the beginning of 1981 had visions of something far greater than a guerrilla force welled up in their minds; something more nearly akin to a conquering army of righteousness. Ronald Reagan, who had campaigned on a straight conservative Republican line was in the White House, probably the first President in American history who had proudly declared himself a conservative, instead of some variation of liberal or progressive. In Britain Margaret Thatcher, also conservative, seemingly had a tight grasp of the Prime Ministership. In several countries on the Continent, starting perhaps with West Germany, conservative parties were showing distinct signs of political prosperity.

In the United States jubilation was especially marked. For Reagan's election could be reasonably regarded as the capstone of a conservative structure that had been building up for thirty years, one that was not only political in character but also cultural and intellectual, that had come to include in its roster names of prominent intellectuals, journals of national circulation and influence, conservative centers and institutes, long known to liberals but rarely to conservatives. A genuine conservative network existed. Most important perhaps the very word *conservative* had become an accepted symbol in the political discourse of the time.

This was indeed an accomplishment. 'Conservative' and 'conservatism' had never been especially popular in American political thought and writing. Unlike Britain which had a Conservative Party to offer ready sanction to conservative impulses, America had only its two major parties and an assortment of small, inconsequential parties of movements built around special interests. In none of the latter did 'conservative' figure. As for the Republican and Democratic parties it was a toss-up prior to the New Deal which had the larger number of conservatives, traditionalists and reactionaries. After all, it was an American boast that the genius of American politics had kept the main line parties on the straight and narrow, each a house of many ideological mansions.

Perhaps it was the lack, or at least faintness, of a feudal tradition in this country, replete with divisions of social class, that prevented from coming into being the kinds of sharp ideological divisions which were common in Europe. The numbers of clamant radicals were relatively low and so were those of the professed political right. Ringing changes on 'liberal' and 'progressive' was a much commoner pursuit in this country. Even 'radical' had an acceptance in politics and religion, and certainly in technology and industry, that 'conservative' lacked.

Yet there was no dearth of Americans who believed dependably in the conservative verities: a minimal state, a strong but unobtrusive government, *laissez-faire* in most matters, family, neighborhood, local community, church and other mediating groups to meet most crises, decentralization, localism, and a preference for tradition and experience over rationalist planning, and withal an unconquerable prejudice against redistributionist measures. This was the conservatism of Presidents like Cleveland, Taft, Coolidge, Hoover, Eisenhower, and of such other American statesmen as Robert Taft, Barry Goldwater and Ronald Reagan during the three decades leading to 1980. At the very bottom of the Great Depression, 17,000,000 Americans endorsed pretty much these ideas when they voted for Landon in 1936. But until 1980, the same ideas seemed to be perennial building blocks of another of America's lost causes, like the Old South and populist agrarianism. Goldwater's defeat in 1964 understandably persuaded a great many Americans that political conservatism was ready for a museum.

Nor was there in America a visible and accepted cultural conservatism as there was in Europe, where one could be a firm conservative in politics and a famous poet or novelist, accepted widely as a creative, even radical mind in literary pursuits: like Eliot, Joyce, Yeats, Mauriac, Mann and others. In the U.S. when a Robert Frost, a Faulkner, or Cozzens came along, critics were unprepared, even resentful in the beginning. In Europe a considerable literature testified to the continuing power of themes of race, family, church, class and region in individual lives and to unresolvable conflicts between the claims of authority and the temptations of freedom. Whatever inclination there may have been before the Civil War in America, in the age of Hawthorne and Melville, toward a comparable community of feeling on authority, evil and punishment, largely disappeared afterwards, leaving a climate of individualism and escape from authority, or else its easy conquest.

There was no more of a conservative climate for scholarship, philosophy and letters after the Civil War, when the forces of populism, frontier-radicalism and competition were dominant. By the early twentieth century in the U.S. it was a rare conservative indeed who inhabited the halls of learning in the universities and colleges across the land. Santayana may have been the only important exception, and he departed Harvard early, to spend his life in Europe. In scholarship the formidable learning and insight of Irving Babbitt and Paul Elmer More were known for the most part by their students alone, one of whom, T. S. Eliot, was quick to escape from his native America to English tradition and authority.

H. L. Mencken was an unabashed conservative in all important respects. He loathed (and wrote against) socialism, social democracy, and all forms of populism. His general contempt for politicians rose to its greatest heights for liberal-democrats like Wilson and Franklin Roosevelt; by *booboisie* he essentially meant all who followed William Jennings Bryan. Mencken was a firm and enthusiastic believer in the rights of property and social class and of the intrinsic wickedness of any kind of redistribution by political means. That Mencken prospered as social critic up to the Depression is probably best explained by the fact that polarizations in politics were not great among intellectuals then, and by his deserved reputation for scorn of Christianity. When, after about 1932, political ideology became vital in the cultural community, and when Mencken's abiding conservatism was fully recognized for the first time, he was reduced to ignominy.

Thus when Lionel Trilling made his notable comment in 1950 about the paucity of conservatives in American intellectual life, he spoke from perspicacity; and when he added that such paucity did not mean there were no strong impulses toward conservatism and even reaction, he showed prescience. For even as Trilling spoke, a conservative renaissance was building. Hayek's *Road to Serfdom* had appeared in 1944 and was getting surprising attention. Richard Weaver's *Ideas Have Consequences* was published in 1948 to generally favorable reviews in this country and the following year Peter Viereck's *Conservatism Revisited* was published.

In the three years 1950–3 in America a small harvest of conservative writings came off the presses. Russell Kirk's *The Conservative Mind* gave scholarly and timely pedigree to conservatism in England and the United States, demonstrating the key role of Burke in both countries. His book was the subject of a *Time* magazine cover story. So was Eric Voegelin's *The New Science of Politics,* a powerful criticism of the liberal mind in political thought. William F. Buckley, *God and Man at Yale,* also received national attention, as did his founding of the distinctly conservative *National Review* not long after. There were other notable books in this three-year period: Gertrude Himmelfarb's *Lord Acton,* Leo Strauss' *Natural Right and History,* John Hallowell's *The Moral Foundations of Democracy* and Daniel Boorstin's *The Genius of American Politics* among them. My *Quest for Community* came out in 1953; I had not particularly written it as a conservative book, but when it was so judged, I did not appeal. By the end of the 1950s the names of Hugh Kenner, Cleanth Brooks, James Burnham and Wilhelm Ropke, were ascendant as scholars and as conservatives in politics. So were the names of the economists Mises, Hayek, Haberler, Fellner and Milton Friedman.

This flood of conservative writing had a fitting context—in England and France as well as in the U.S. In England the names of Christopher Dawson, Freya Stark, Malcolm Muggeridge and Michael Oakeshott did not suggest renascence so much as a steady continuation of a well-established conservative tradition. The same was true of Jacques Ellul, Bertrand de Jouvenel and Raymond Aron in France. All of these authors were well known in America. Conservative journals, led by Buckley's *National Review,* began to appear on the American scene in the 1950s among them *Modern Age* and *The Intercollegiate Review,* the last witness to the gathering conservative movement on college campuses. Henry Regnery proved that a forthrightly conservative publisher of conservative books could be commercially successful. The American Enterprise Institute and The Hoover Institution, founded earlier, came alive in the 1950s and would become models for dozens of other institutes during the next two decades. A few conservative foundations came cautiously on the scene to seek to rival the massive Ford Foundation in the distribution of fellowships and grants. All in all, the conservative renascence was well under way by the end of the 1950s.

Helping it was the unforeseen religious revival of the decade on the campuses in America. Speakers were demanded—Tillich, Niebuhr, Bishop Sheen, Billy Graham and many others. The impetus came almost exclusively from students, and faculties were generally embarrassed at the time. After all, had it not been conclusively proved that rationalism was sovereign and religion on the way to history's dust bin? Had the underground rumblings of a far greater religious renascence, that of the evangelicals in the South and South-west, reached the ears of academics and other intellectuals in the 1950s, they would have been made apprehensive indeed. I realize that religion can be the hand maiden of liberalism and radicalism as well as conservatism, but the direction in the 1950s, on and off campuses, was generally conservative.

Two other developments, also fortuitous, gave substantial aid to the burgeoning conservative cause. I refer to the resurrections of Alexis de Tocqueville and Edmund Burke throughout the decade. Both had languished in this country prior to the Second World War. In seven years of a better than average undergraduate and graduate education at Berkeley in the 1930s, I never once heard Tocqueville referred to and Burke was limited to something called the 'organic school.' But this changed remarkably beginning in the late 1940s. A new edition by Knopf of *Democracy in America* came out in 1945, and its attraction was immediate. Paperback editions and printings of this book and also of *The Old Regime and the French Revolution* were legion by the end of the 1950s. 'As Tocqueville says' came to rival 'as Marx says' in faculty clubs. Predictably, the political left tried to appropriate Tocqueville, finding some kind of Baconian cryptogram no doubt, but Tocqueville's proper linkage to conservatism was nevertheless fully recognized in the 1950s.

Burke's resurrection was less notable and widely felt perhaps but it was impressive. He became known, chiefly through Kirk's *Conservative Mind,* as the founder, the Karl Marx, of Western conservatism, and even his *Reflections on the Revolution in France,* once almost abhorred in American academic and intellectual communities, became the object of a considerable number of printings. The 20-year project of his *Collected Letters* by the University of Chicago Press began in the 1950s. An impressive number of anthologies, textbook paperback printings, and scholarly commentaries changed Burke's once lack-luster status in America.

Neo-conservatism was born in and of the 1960s. It cannot be separated from the prior rise of the New Left and the outbreak of the Student Revolution of the decade. Irving Kristol, a central figure in the development, once described a Neo-conservative as a liberal mugged by the Revolution. The New Left, in America at least, was primarily a campus phenomenon in the beginning, and so was Neo-conservatism. From the perspective of this book, a kind of historical cunning must be ascribed to Neo-conservatism, for it was but the latest of a sequence, starting with Burke's *Reflections* of reactive relationships between conservatism and turmoil.

It is not surprising that a considerable number of previously liberal and social democratic faculty members should have turned to the political right by the late 1960s. After all, much of the fury of the revolution on the campus was directed, or seemed to be at the time, toward, not conservatives or reactionaries, such as they were, but to liberals. The spectacular rebellions at Berkeley, Cornell, Wisconsin, Harvard, Yale, Michigan, and other major universities were almost without exception rebellions against liberal presidents and predictably liberal faculty senates and committees. Conservative scholars—who were not numerous and may simply have been overlooked—were rarely harassed by the New Left on the campuses. The most insistent and prolonged campaigns by the Left were preceded by a wide range of indulgences and grants of amnesty, of doctrinal nourishment and proffers of refuge. It was as though the student revolutionists, in Freudian enactment of primordial passion, chose to kill the very fathers in many instances of their movement on campus—those of the faculty who had from the beginning nurtured and protected them.

By the mid-1960s the Student Revolution was sufficiently advanced in America, sufficiently destructive of the academic community—including authority over curriculum and freedom from persecution in classroom and office—as to invite the beginning of a decidedly conservative reaction. Articles began to appear in which

words *authority, civil order, tradition* and *social contract* were prominent.

Thus were born the Neo-conservatives who could mostly be said
to have followed the example of Burke in letting a revolution be the
precipitating condition of their doctrine. It was the socialist Michael
Harrington who gave Neoconservatism its name and who wanted
none of it for himself. From the start the leading figure among
Neoconservatives was Irving Kristol. He had never been in any solid
sense a liberal. From youthful Trotskyism he went directly to an
eclectic political philosophy that was generally more skeptical than
receptive of modernity. He had cofounded with Stephen Spender
Encounter in 1955 and done a great deal of writing in the years
leading up to his cofounding with Daniel Bell of *The Public Interest*
in 1965—the journal most closely linked to Neo-conservatism,
though *Commentary* under Norman Podhoretz and *Encounter* under Melvin Lasky should not be overlooked in this respect.

One must exercise a certain tact in identifying the principal Neo-
conservatives of the 1960s and 1970s for not all of them were willing to accept the label, preferring in some cases continuation of the
political identity they had known all their lives. But with this qualifi-
cation in mind, the names of Daniel Patrick Moynihan, Nathan Glazer,
Daniel Bell, Seymour Martin Lipset, Samuel Huntington and James
Q. Wilson, were high among the most often-cited of the
Neoconservatives. No matter how stoutly they may today deny ac-
curacy of the Neo-conservative identity given them in those years,
in retrospect it is as though by some invisible hand their writings and
lectures gave help to the conservatives' cause when it was needed.

The two conservatisms, New and Neo, had important likenesses
of idea and judgement. In common was a fullblown antipathy to the
New Left and to the 'establishment' liberalism of the Galbraiths and
Schlesingers, the Kennedys and McGoverns. There was from the
beginning in each conservatism a sophisticated awareness of the
real strengths of Soviet Communism in the world and a disposition
to counter-attack. In both there is substantial suspicion and distrust
of the kind of nationalization and centralization of state and economy
that had become a staple in much liberalism and social democracy.
Correspondingly, we find a fresh interest in the remaining virtues of
localism and regionalism in an increasingly national and interna-
tional economy in the West; there is a common interest in the mecha-

nisms of the free market, for long somewhat disregarded by economists overwhelmingly Keynesian in perspective, in the role of public judgement in critical issues as compared with that of rationalist-
oriented bureaucrats. There was in both sets of ideas a novel respect
for Congress and the Judiciary after so many years of liberal adulation of the White House.

There were differences: greater interest by New Conservatives in
religious and moral objectives; greater affection among most Neo-
conservatives for the aims if not the currently operating procedures
of the welfare state. There was and is broader evidence of a socialist or social democratic subconscious in the Neo- than the
New Conservative whose roots tended to be conservative. Nevertheless, these differences accepted, it remains a fact that by
1980 the media often used 'neo-conservative' and 'conservative'
interchangeably.

Reagan's victory in 1980 was widely hailed as a conservative triumph, and in a considerable degree it was. For a quarter of a century
he had been widely known in America as an apostle of full-blown
political and economic conservatism. If there was also a noticeable
streak of populism—one that would constantly widen in his Presi-
dency—it harmonized well with conservative dogma, as it did in
Margaret Thatcher in Britain.

Reagan's triumph, though, was one of a coalition of persuasions,
some of which had at very best an uneasy relationship with conservatism of any kind. It was the greatest coalition victory since Franklin
Roosevelt's in 1932. Jeane Kirkpatrick gave it the name of the Reagan
Phenomenon, likening it to FDR's in its sweep and multiplicity of
substance. No one back in the 1930s called FDR's coalition 'Liberal;' not with the Deep South a key part of it. 'Progressive' and
'New Deal' were the common labels for FDR's coalition.

It was different from the beginning with the Reagan coalition.
Conservative was the word for the coalition, for its leading figures,
and for each and every act—the only real limit put on the use of the
word being the degree of conservative; i.e. 'hard-line,' 'pragmatic,'
and the like. The criteria of these degrees shifted from month to
month, but once an individual was labeled at all, he was labeled for
good. To the end of his/her days, the label would stick. Reagan was
an authentic conservative in the American idiom, but as President he

was a good deal more: populist, evangelical, Far Rightist, and so on, by turns and doubtless by calculation.

Reaganite forces were polyglot indeed. The Far Right, veterans of the Goldwater campaign in 1964, were interested in one thing—to capture and hold power; the evangelicals, eager to implement by law, even constitutional amendment, had such moral goals as the prohibition of abortion, and the opening of public schools to prayers; the libertarians were willing to suffer Reagan's moral and social views for his attitude on taxes; the populists saw in Reagan's charisma the driving force for attainment of an ever-more-direct democracy; partisans of a more aggressive foreign policy and defense build-up; and old-line conservatives who abominated big budgets and bureaucracies, and who were by nature suspicious of not only populists but also the commerce threatening, budget-expanding enthusiasts for great increases in military expenditures. All of these were pronounced 'conservative.'

Of all the *mis*ascriptions of the word 'conservative' during the last four years, the most amusing, in an historical light, is surely the application of 'conservative' to the last-named. For in America throughout the twentieth century, and including four substantial wars abroad, conservatives had been steadfastly the voices of non-inflationary military budgets, and of an emphasis on trade in the world instead of American nationalism. In the two World Wars, in Korea, and in Viet Nam, the leaders of American entry into war were such renowned liberal-progressives as Woodrow Wilson, Franklin Roosevelt, Harry Truman and John F. Kennedy. In all four episodes conservatives, both in the national government and in the rank and file, were largely hostile to intervention; were isolationists indeed.

The picture is more complex in British history, and I will not generalize. But it is useful to remember that in the 1930s the whole policy of British appeasement was identified with Conservatives. In America things may be changing now, but in the past, unfailingly, liberals, progressives and social democrats have proved more reliable as followers of Wilson, FDR, and Kennedy than have fiscal conservatives. Irving Kristol has written that 'traditional conservatism, in our century at least, will blow the patriotic bugles at appropriate occasions, but it is far less interested in foreign policy than in economics.' Tocqueville noted as one of democracy's weaknesses—in a world of hostile powers—the reluctance of the middle class to abandon commerce and profit for necessary preparation for war.

Liberals and social democrats like death and destruction no more than do conservatives. But they like some of the accompaniments of large-scale war: the opportunities created for central planning of economy, for pre-emption of legislative functions, and other pursuits dear to the hearts of political rationalists and enthusiasts. President Reagan's deepest soul is not Republican-conservative but New Deal Second World War Democrat. Thus his well noted preference for citing FDR and Kennedy as noble precedents for his actions rather than Coolidge, Hoover, or even Eisenhower. The word 'revolution' springs lightly from his lips, for anything from tax reform to narcotics prosecution.

Reagan's passion for crusades, moral and military, is scarcely American-conservative. Conservatives dislike government on our backs, and Reagan duly echoes this dislike, but he echoes more enthusiastically the Moral Majority's crusade to put more government on our backs, i.e. a moral-inquisitorial government well armed with constitutional amendments, laws and decrees. Moral Majoritarians do not like governmental power less because they cherish Christian morality more—a characteristic they share with those Revolution-supporting clerics in France and England to whom Burke gave the labels of 'political theologians' and 'theological politicians,' not, obviously, liking either.

From the traditional conservative's point of view it is fatuous to use the family—as the evangelical crusaders regularly do—as the justification for their tireless crusades to ban abortion categorically, to bring the Department of Justice in on every Baby Doe, to mandate by constitution the imposition of 'voluntary' prayers in the public schools, and so on. From Burke on it has been a conservative precept and a sociological principle since Auguste Comte that the surest way of weakening the family, or any vital social group, is for the government to assume, and then monopolize, the family's historic functions.

So is there open, sometimes bitter, conflict between conservative and populist. Populism, by its history and current ideology, is essentially a radical persuasion, one aimed at a leveling of elite bodies from AT&T to Harvard University. Its utopian dream is the conservative's nightmare: a society in which all constitutional limitations upon the direct power of the people, or any passing majority, are abrogated, leaving something akin to the mystique of Rousseau's General Will. At the present time, the hated enemies of populists are the Supreme Court and the Federal Reserve Bank.

The Far Right is less interested in Burkean immunities from government power than it is in putting a maximum of governmental power in the hands of those who can be trusted. It is control of power, not diminution of power, that ranks high. Thus when Reagan was elected conservatives hoped for the quick abolition of such government 'monstrosities' as the Department of Energy, the Department of Education, and the two National Endowments of the Arts and Humanities, all creations of the political left. The Far Right in the Reagan Phenomenon saw it differently, however; they saw it as an opportunity for retaining and enjoying the powers. And the Far Right prevailed. It seeks to prevail also in the establishment of a 'national industrial strategy,' a government corporation structure in which the conservative dream of free private enterprise would be extinguished.

One of the consequences of the Reagan Phenomenon has been the onset of a compulsive fascination with *authenticity* and *inauthenticity;* this is well known in modern religious and revolutionary history. Nothing was more important to the early Protestant than that his faith, directly in God alone, unmediated by pagan-Roman externalities and distractions, be authentic and be regarded by others as authentic: that is, sincere, complete and unmixed with ulterior motive or ambition. Hypocrisy was for some time the deadliest of sins in the Protestant theodicy.

This intensity of faith, passion for authenticity, passed into religion-related politics in the seventeenth century, notably among the Puritans during the Civil War in England. By the time of the French Revolution the politics of *la patrie* had reached a religious fervor, to be seen among the Jacobins in a constantly growing measure. By the height of the Revolution in 1793–4 the passion for authenticity was almost uncontrollable among the revolutionaries. The Revolution began to devour its own, keeping the guillotine working overtime in the execution of even high officials like Robespierre for the crime of 'hypocrisy' or 'inauthenticity.'

There are no guillotines on Capitol Hill or the Mall in Washington, but there are punishments for the 'inauthentic' and rewards for the 'authentic.' Struggles for the mythical award of The Truest Conservative of the Month, have increased in scope and intensity during the last two years. Suspicions lie everywhere, just as they came to among Jacobins. They may suddenly touch someone thought to be 'pragmatic' instead of 'hard line;' or they may land on the Moral Majoritarian whose conscience forbids his going all the way in the categorical anathema upon abortion; or it might be the Congressmen, previously thought safe, who makes budget deficits more important than a measureless national military defense. It is impossible to know in advance.

If the mirror on the wall of fairy-tale origin were to be made actual in today's Washington, it would be worth creating a state lottery for the variant answers that would come to the question, who is the fairest conservative of them all? It might today be the individual who has just called for War in Central America; tomorrow the most indefatigable picket before abortion hospitals and where Baby Does are born; the next day it might well be the populist instigator of some scheme for fiscal egalitarianism. We cannot be certain. Except of one thing: it will never be the conservative who traces ancestry back through Goldwater, Taft, Cleveland, all the way to John Adams and Edmund Burke.

What, then, is the probable fate of the conservative and his ideology, once the Reagan Phenomenon cracks-up? No political leader, not Ronald Reagan, not FDR, not even a Lloyd George or Churchill could hold together for very long the polyglot assemblage that has made up the Reagan Phenomenon since 1980. The disintegration of the Phenomenon—and it is already under way—will throw each of the highly disparate persuasions back upon its old resources, there to plot no doubt fresh alliances toward yet another coalition of victory under yet another charismatic politician if he can be found.

Traditional conservatism is one of these persuasions; it too will find itself back in something of, though not entirely, its old position of gadfly, critic, and occasional gatherer of the spoils. But, as far as one can judge, it will not be altogether the same old position. For in truth, conservatism has left discernible prints upon the sand during its 30-year renaissance in America. It has, with the aid of the Neoconservatives, moved the political spectrum at least somewhat to the right. Its by now widely publicized taunts of liberals and social democrats as bureaucracy-builders and centralizing collectiv-

ists have left their mark. Liberals are as quick as conservatives today
to declare abhorrence of 'throwing money at' political and social
problems. Most important, in a news-saturated society, the labels
'conservative' and 'conservatism,' for action and philosophy respec-
tively, are firmly planted.

Nor should we forget the long-held advantage of conservatism in
the West: its clear hold upon the symbols and mystiques of *family,
local community, parish, neighborhood,* and *mutual-aid* groups of
all types. The conservative philosophy was born of Burke's and others' antagonism to the deadly *étatisme* and *individualisme* which
had, like pincers, threatened to crush the traditional intermediate
groups in the social order. From these verities sprang inevitably a
high premium upon the values of localism and decentralization, of
the private sector generally, and upon a government concerned with
its inherent constitutional responsibilities instead of dozens and hundreds of social and economic entitlements.

The residual strength of a doctrine or creed is often best shown by
the tribute paid it, however falsely or hypocritically, by its adversar-
ies. Such conservative words as *family, kin, neighborhood* and *community* have long held appeal to the political clerisy in the West—
evidenced by the frequent use as euphemisms of these words for the
state and its commands. In 1984, at the Democratic Convention in
San Francisco, Governor Cuomo made use of 'family' some two
dozen times; not, however, in reference to the household but to the
whole American nation. 'Community' and 'wagon train' were other
homely traditionalisms the Governor saw fit to use as fig leaves for
the naked public square. Quite apart from symbolic value and even
genuine, concrete reference, family, kindred, neighborhood and locality, even region and race, have a universal historical meaning that is
not likely to be entirely eroded away by the acids of modernity.

It is possible that traditional conservatism will be strengthened by
what is increasingly being hailed as Welfare Conservatism, a product in considerable measure of the work of the Neo-conservatives.
Some conservatives doubtless draw back from the phrase, likening
it in their minds to such oxymorons as *'laissez-faire* socialism' or
'authoritarian liberalism.' But the future of the welfare state, barring
utter catastrophe in the world, is thoroughly assured by now. Early
in the century Sir William Harcourt felt obliged to say, 'We're all
socialists now.' We can say much the same of citizens of the welfare

state today; we all belong. The fateful inclusion of the middle class and its values and desires in the welfare state, making it today by far the largest beneficiary, meant that real opposition to it was a thing of the past. The assurance of a generous Social Security and Medicare entitlement, and without means-testing, together with annual subsidies to farmers, small businesses, and to the huge educational establishment, the largesse that now extends to substantial aid for college students and to vast bailouts for giant corporations, the creation of large endowments at taxpayer expense for support of the arts, the humanities, and most recently political philosophy, all this and a great deal more make up the dominant reality today of the welfare state. Sadly, even tragically, the epithet 'welfare' or 'welfare state' continues to be fixed in the public mind as the sum of benefits received by the impoverished and disabled; for the truth is, the money going to these groups is but a fraction of the public revenue that does to the middle and upper classes.

Therefore, to become and be known as a Welfare Conservative will not affect current reality much in political campaigns. The great objective of Welfare Conservatives at the moment is establishing a lustrous pedigree; hence the mutilations of history in their futile hope of making Burke, Disraeli and Bismarck their ancestors. They might better be exploring the ways by which they can maintain an identity separate from that of liberals and neo-liberals.

A substantial core of traditional conservatism will continue to exist in both England and the United States. A political faith that is two centuries old does not extinguish easily. The Renaissance of 1950–80 will be a constant and kindly light for conservative dreams. If it happened once, why not again? Moreover, there is vital need for a politics of the past; that is, a political ideology built around the study as well as evocation of the past. It has yet to be proved that futurism is more than fanciful rhetoric based upon hunches. But the past in all its boundless diversity, is *there*. The new, as art and science as well as a business teaches us, is accomplished by new arrangements of the 'usable past,' as Eliot called it, arrangements which, when made superlatively well, generate novel forces.

There is no necessary antagonism between devotion to past and attention to present. Churchill by his own admission loved the past, disliked the present, and feared the future. He coped adequately, to say the least, as did Disraeli and Bismarck, with the present.

Traditional conservatives have, and will continue to have, a good deal in common with the socialists in the democracies. The socialists too, though for different reasons, reject the present and, in an interesting way, enjoy the past—that is, the special past formed by Marx, by Marx's mental picture of the past, and by the whole past that was occupied so happily until about the Second World War by socialists in the world's intellectual hierarchy. The socialists have, just as do traditional conservatives, a complete and self-sufficient program for all seasons, which is something liberals, who tend to live in hand-and-mouth ideological circumstances, do not and never will have. There were figures in nineteenth-century Europe whose special uses of the moral, esthetic, technological and political pasts make it difficult to place them as traditionalists or radicals. Proudhon was emphatically radical, but he made the patriarchal family and the autonomous village basic to his anarchism. Dostoevsky was traditionalist, but his merciless assaults on modernity and Westernism in Russia were inevitably of service to radicals.

Both sets of traditionalists—Burkean conservatives and Marxian socialists—are compelled to live under the liberal welfare state, which they do not like, though for different reasons, and both ideological groups will yield, as they have for some time now, culture-guerrillas whose most obvious future is that of use of the past in attack on the present.

A Bibliographical Note

Two books by Russell Kirk offer an admirable introduction to the history and major texts of Anglo-American conservatives: *The Conservative Mind* and *The Portable Conservative Reader.* On German conservatism, primarily of the early nineteenth century, Karl Mannheim's 'Conservative Thought' in his *Essays on Sociology and Social Psychology,* is valuable. On the early French conservatives, John T. Mertz, *History of European Thought in the Nineteenth Century* (the fourth volume, on society), is helpful as are the chapters on Bonald, Lammennais, Brunetiere and Bourget in Harold Laski, *Authority in the Modern State.* My own *Social Group in French Thought* deals with the early French conservatives and their followers in law and social reform. Peter Viereck, *Conservatism Revisited,* is recommended for its compact union of analytical and historical aspects.

The following lists the major conservatives and works on which my treatment in this volume is largely based. Burke, *Reflections on the Revolution in France* primarily, but also his speeches on the American colonists, the British East India Company, and Ireland, and also the less known but highly illuminating *Thoughts and Details on Scarcity,* as close to a formal work on political economy as Burke ever came.

FRENCH: Louis de Bonald, *Theorie du Pouvoir* and *Legislation Primitive,* both contained in his *Oeuvres Completes* (translations of Bonald are few); Joseph de Maistre, *Considerations on France* and *Generative Principles of Constitutions* (see the excellent anthology of de Maistre by Jack Lively); Hugues Felicite de Lamennais, *Essai sur lIndifference* and *Paroles du Croyant;* Renee de Chateaubriand, *The Genius of Christianity;* Alexis de Tocqueville, *Democracy in America, The Old Regime and the French Revolution,* and *Recollections;* Paul Bourget, *Studies;* Bertrand de Jouvenel, *The Ethics of Redistribution* and *Power;* Jacques Ellul, *The Political Illusion* and *The Technological Society.*

ENGLISH: Samuel T. Coleridge, *The Constitution of Church and State;* Robert Southey, *Letters from England;* Benjamin Disraeli, *A Vindication of the Constitution* and either *Sybil* or *Coningsby* from his novels (Robert Blake's fine biography of Disraeli is the best and shortest way to his subject's political philosophy); Henry Maine, *Popular Government;* T. S. Eliot, *Idea of a Christian Society;* Christopher Dawson, *Religion and the Modern State;* Michael Oakeshott, *Rationalism in Politics.*

AMERICAN: John Adams, *Defence of Constitutions of Government;* Alexander Hamilton, *The Stand,* a distinctly Burkean reaction to the French Revolution among other things; *The Federalist;* James Fenimore Cooper, *The American Democrat;* Orestes Brownson: the best introduction to this extraordinary mind is Russell Kirk, *Orestes Brownson: Select Essays;* E. L. Godkin, *Problems of Modern Democracy;* Henry Adams, *The Education of Henry Adams;* Brooks Adams, *The Law of Civilization and Decay;* Irving Babbitt, *Democracy and Leadership* and *Rousseau and Romanticism;* Paul Elmer More, see his *Shelburne Essays,* passim; Russell Kirk, *A Program for Conservatives;* William F. Buckley, *Up From Liberalism;* Richard Weaver, *Ideas Have Consequences;* Peter Viereck, *Conservatism Revisited;* Robert Nisbet, *Twilight of Authority* and *Prejudices: A Philosophical Dictionary;* Irving Kristol, *Reflections of a Neoconservative.*

GERMAN: Karl Ludwig Haller, *The Restoration of the Social Sciences;* G. W. F. Hegel, *Philosophy of Right;* Wilhelm von Humboldt, *The Sphere and Duties of Government;* Otto von Gierke, *German Law of Associations;* Oswald Spengler, *The Decline of the West;* Eric Voegelin, *Order and History* and *The New Science of Politics;* Wilhelm Röpke, *The Social Crisis of Our Time.*

Dates and Nationalities of Principal Conservatives Mentioned in Text

Chateaubriand, Francois Auguste 1768–1848, French; Coleridge, Samuel Taylor 1772–1834, English; Comte, Auguste 1798–1857, French; Dawson, Christopher 1880–1970, English; Disraeli, Benjamin 1804–81, English; Eliot, T. S. 1888–1965, American-English; Gierke, Otto von 1844–1921, German; Haller, Karl Ludwig von 1768–1854, German; Hayek, Friedrich von 1899–, German–English; Hegel, Georg Wilhelm Friedrich 1770–1831, German; Inge, William R. 1860–1954, English; Jouvenel, Bertrand de 1903–, French; Kirk, Russell 1918–, American; Le Play, Pierre G. Frederic 1806–82, French; Maine, Henry 1822–88, English; Maistre, Joseph de 1753–1821, French; Mannheim, Karl 1893–1947, Austro-Hungarian; Mencken, Henry L. 1880–1956, American; More, Paul E. 1864–1937, American; Newman, John Henry 1801–90, English; Oakeshott, Michael 1901–, English; Ostrogorski, Moisey Y. 1854–1919, Russian; Randolph, John 1773–1833, American; Saint–Simon, Claude–Henri 1760–1825, French; Santayana, George 1863–1952, American; Savigny, Friedrich Karl von 1779–1861, German; Schumpeter, Joseph 1883–1950, Austrian–American; Southey, Robert 1774–1843, English; Tocqueville, Alexis de 1805–59, French; Viereck, Peter 1916–, American; Weaver, Richard 1910–63, American.

Index

CPSIA information can be obtained
at www.ICGtesting.com
Printed in the USA
FSHW020001010519
57724FS